A Concise Guide to the

Seashore

A CONCISE GUIDE TO THE
SEASHORE

Patrick Hook

Bath · New York · Singapore · Hong Kong · Cologne · Delhi · Melbourne

First published by Parragon in 2008

Parragon Books Ltd
Queen Street House
4 Queen Street
Bath, BA1 1HE

Produced by Focus Publishing
Designer Philip Clucas
Project Editor Guy Croton
Indexer Caroline Watson

See page 256 for photograph
copyright details
Text © Parragon Books Ltd 2008

ISBN 978-1-4075-1134-4
Printed in China

CONTENTS

INTRODUCTION 10

SEASHELLS 32–65

SEA SLUGS 66–71

CEPHALOPODS 72–81

CRUSTACEANS 82–105

SEA ANEMONES & SEA PENS
106–113

JELLYFISH 114–121

ECHINODERMS 122–139

FISH 140–149

SEAWEEDS, SPONGES & CORALLINES 150–163

TRUE WORMS 164–169

FLOWERING PLANTS 170–187

BIRDS 188–205

REPTILES 206–215

AMPHIBIANS 216–221

MAMMALS 222–229

INSECTS & OTHER
INVERTEBRATES 230–245

INTRODUCTION

The definition of exactly what comprises the seashore can vary significantly. At its most basic, it can be considered to be the area between the high and low tide marks. This view, however, misses out on a vast component of what is one of the most fascinating and complex ecosystems on the planet. The approach taken in this book encompasses the range of habitats that are intimately connected with the actions of the tides. This covers four distinct areas; the undercliff and any dune systems, marshes or lakes behind the shoreline, the narrow fringe of land above the high tide mark that is directly affected by the sea's spray, the tidal zone itself, and the sub-tidal region immediately below it.

Although the seashore is visited by countless millions of people every year, very few of them take the opportunity to study the life forms found there. This is a great shame, as the potential for capturing the imagination – especially that of young people – is tremendous. An excellent way to start finding out about coastal plants and animals is through beachcombing – searching for objects that have been washed up by the sea, and working out what they are. Rockpools are even better places to examine; poking through seaweed and looking under rocks can reveal all manner of unexpected treasures. This book therefore sets out to present the reader with a concise guide to all the wonders of the seashore.

The Zones of the Seashore

The Supra-Littoral Zone

The supra-littoral zone is the area immediately above the highest tide line – it is the strip of land that is directly affected by spray from the sea, but not submerged under it. Above this zone is a less well-defined fringe that is also intimately associated with the salt-laden air that blows off the sea.

The supra-littoral zone.

The Littoral Zone

The littoral zone is the area that lies between the high water and low water marks. Organisms that live in it are subject to the powerful action of the waves as well as constantly changing conditions due to the movement of the tides. Survival is therefore extremely challenging, and evolution has consequently produced many different ecological adaptations. In spite of the hardships, the littoral zone often teems with all manner of strange and wonderful creatures.

The littoral zone.

The Sublittoral Zone

The sublittoral zone lies just below the low water mark – technically, it is defined as reaching down to 200 metres (656 ft) below sea level. However, for the purposes of this book, it is considered to be the region that can be easily accessed by the visitor whilst snorkelling. It is home to many animals and plants that are not able to live in the tidal zone, and is therefore well worth examination.

The sublittoral zone.

The Supra-Littoral Zone and Other Habitats Above the High Water Mark

Many different habitats can be found immediately above the high water mark. These can include shingle banks, sand dunes, rocks, undercliff strips, cliffs, estuaries, mud flats and salt marshes. The creatures and plants found in these habitats may include large numbers of species that are also found further inland. Others, however, may only be able to survive in these specialized environments.

The Sea Slater can only be found in the supra-littoral zone, having evolved exclusively in this specialized environment.

Hottentot figs grow both on the seashore and inland.

Shingle Banks

Shingle banks do not offer much in the way of cover, except for those creatures which are small enough to find their way into the nooks and crannies that lie between the myriads of small stones, or those that live amongst the piles of tidal flotsam. Small invertebrates such as sand hoppers and sea slaters often abound in this habitat, and can usually be exposed by scraping away a few layers of shingle or turning over dead seaweed. Although they are rarely seen during the day, at night they come out of hiding and feed on tidal refuse. In some areas there can be as many as 25,000 per square metre. There are also several species of insect that feed on rotting seaweed – examples include various species of kelp fly. These medium-sized flies wait until after the spring high tide and then lay their eggs on the piles of seaweed that accumulate high on the beach. The eggs then hatch and the resulting larvae eat the decomposing vegetation – in doing so, they help to recycle nutrients back into the environment. Further down on the size scale, vast numbers of tiny spider mites also swarm over the assorted tidal debris – they are both scavengers and predators, and will exploit more or less any feeding opportunity that presents itself.

Sand Dunes

Sand dunes can vary in size from small piles of sand a few metres high, to towering hills accumulated over tens of thousands of years. The plants that live on sand dunes are often highly specialized to deal with the harsh conditions, where high wind speeds and a lack of fresh water are major constraints to survival. Marram grass is a good example of a plant that has successfully adapted to this ecological niche. It has long root systems which provide excellent anchorage as well as sufficient water retention.

Marram grass growing on a sand dune.

Alliums and many other plants thrive on the rocks and cliffs above the seashore.

Rocks and Cliffs

The rocks and cliffs that lie above the high water mark can
be home to various different fauna and flora, depending on
a variety of factors such as overall climate and the amount
of salt spray that gets blown onto them. Many of the plants
that live there have adapted to cope with the sparse soil
and often arid conditions by developing specialized root
systems. These are able to force their way into minute cracks
and crevices and derive sufficient nourishment to survive.
Others, such as lichens, anchor themselves on hard surfaces
and do without any significant root system – as a result of the
lack of nutrients, they are extremely slow-growing. Cliffs
are also important places for many kinds of animals such as
seabirds, which use them as safe roosting and nesting sites.

The Undercliff

The undercliff is a zone that is often found between the shoreline and the cliffs. It is created by geological instability as a result of soft stratas underlying harder ones. As the soft layers get eroded away, the harder ones collapse leaving an area that is often so inaccessible or dangerous that it does not get disturbed by human activity. In some places, the undercliff zone can extend for many miles, creating havens for many types of wildlife.

Undercliffs are inaccessible and dangerous – ideal for species which do not want to be disturbed.

Salt Marshes and Other Places Covered with Vegetation

Estuaries and mud flats are usually fringed with thick vegetation, whereas salt marshes are often more or less entirely covered with plants of one sort or another. These species have evolved to cope with the high salt content of the water, and can usually also survive occasional total immersion. These areas mark a boundary between the marine habitat and that of the land. Since they are relatively inaccessible to the larger land predators such as foxes, they provide safe nesting sites for many species of birds. During the migration seasons of spring and autumn, estuaries provide vital resting and feeding areas for vast numbers of birds. Likewise, those situated in warmer climes also act as sanctuaries for birds that travel south to escape severe polar winters.

The Littoral Zone

Sandy Beaches

Sandy beaches are very difficult places for marine organisms to live as they are constantly shifting – a single storm can remove tens of thousands of tons of sand from a beach in a matter of hours. This usually happens during the harsh weather of winter. The quieter waters of summer then allow the sand to start accumulating again, only for the cycle to be repeated as the seasons change. As a consequence of this, it is not possible for any degree of permanence to be built up, meaning that nothing like rooted plants can establish itself. There are, however, many sand-dwelling creatures that can cope with being constantly washed out to sea. These include certain sand-loving starfish (sea stars), sea urchins and molluscs.

Many species of starfish are able to survive being washed back and forth from sea to beach.

All manner of creatures visit
pebble beaches.

Muddy beaches teem with life and
are extremely important ecosystems.

Pebble and Shingle Beaches

Beaches composed of pebbles or shingle are even harsher
places for flora and fauna to live than those on sandy shores.
Although they have many similar constraints, such as storms
and strong tides being able to change their form overnight,
it is much easier to live in sand than amongst constantly
shifting stones. Consequently, the commonest creatures are
amphipods and other small scavengers.

Muddy Beaches

Muddy beaches may be found along coasts and estuaries the
world over. They are incredibly important ecosystems, as
they are usually covered with a thick sediment that is full
of nutrients. This is mostly derived from organic debris
that has settled to the bottom in the relatively still water.
Microscopic plants such as diatoms form a large proportion
of the biota with many different species being found, but the
number of larger plant species is small. They can, however,
cover vast areas — Sea lettuce (*Ulva expansa*) and Mermaid's

hair (*Enteromorpha tubulosa*) are two of the most commonly seen, and may form extensive beds. This rich feeding ground supports a vast number of small creatures, from marine worms to molluscs and crustaceans. They in turn attract huge numbers of larger creatures – especially birds, such as waders. At high tide the mud flats are covered with water, but become fully exposed to the elements again at low tide.

Estuary Channels

Many mud flats and open sandy areas have deep channels running between them. These attract large numbers of marine creatures as they are usually rich in nutrients and relatively stable environments. They are often lined with eel grass (*Zostera marina*), which provides both food and protection for many small creatures, including pipe fish, seahorse, sand eels, sea slugs and many different shelled molluscs. They are also important breeding grounds for many species of fish, such as sharks, rays, flounder, plaice and mullet.

Opposite and below: Littoral zones.

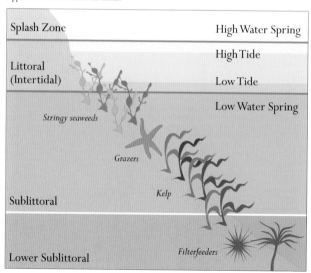

Splash Zone — High Water Spring

Littoral (Intertidal) — High Tide — Low Tide

Low Water Spring

Stringy seaweeds

Grazers

Kelp

Sublittoral

Filterfeeders

Lower Sublittoral

The Tide Zones of a Rocky Shore

The organisms that live in the upper tidal zone of a rocky shore include barnacles, marine algae and certain gastropods such as periwinkles. Further down, limpets and various species of crab may be found, along with sea anemones and starfish. The lowest tidal reaches are home to sea urchins, abalone, sea slugs and many others.

High Tide

Limpet

Sea Anemone

Rockweed

Laminaria

Sea Urchin

Low Tide

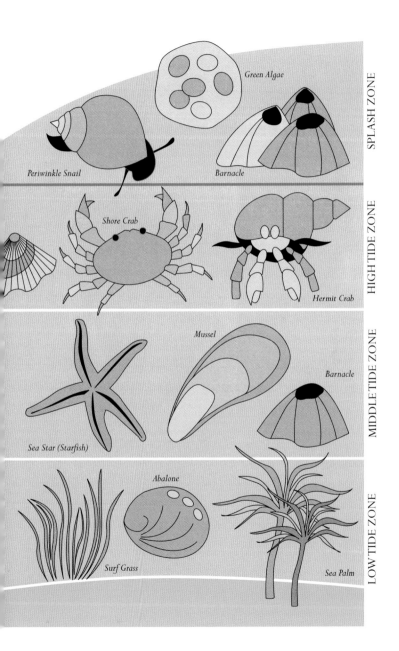

Green Algae

Periwinkle Snail

Barnacle

SPLASH ZONE

Shore Crab

Hermit Crab

HIGH TIDE ZONE

Mussel

Barnacle

Sea Star (Starfish)

MIDDLE TIDE ZONE

Abalone

Surf Grass

Sea Palm

LOW TIDE ZONE

The High Tide Zone

The high tide zone is the area that is only submerged during the highest part of the tide. It is populated with species that are capable of withstanding long periods out of water. These include barnacles and mussels, as well as creatures that are capable of moving up with the tide, and then back again with it when it recedes, such as periwinkles, and so on.

The Mid Tide Zone

The mid tide zone is the area that is submerged halfway between high and low water – since it spends much less time uncovered, there is a far greater variety of animals and plants which can live there. A large proportion of the immobile species only locate themselves in places where they are shaded from the sun – this helps to prevent

Limpets commonly inhabit mid tide zones.

desiccation. Others exploit the rock pools that can often be found in this zone. Examples of mid tide zone organisms include sea anemones, limpets, periwinkles and various species of seaweed.

The Low Tide Zone

The low tide zone is only exposed for a relatively short amount of time. Consequently, there is a far greater diversity of species found there. These include starfish, sea urchins, sea slugs and in the deeper pools even creatures like octopus and flatfish.

The Major Groups

The fauna and flora of the seashore are made up of species from several major groups, these are:

The Molluscs – made up of gastropods, bivalves and cephalopods.

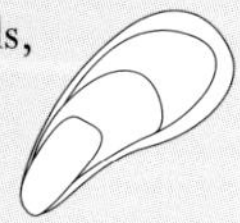

The Crustaceans – crabs, lobsters, shrimps, etc.

The Anthozoans – sea anemones and sea pens.

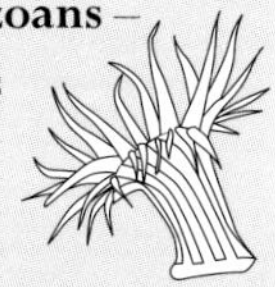

The Scyphozoans – jellyfish.

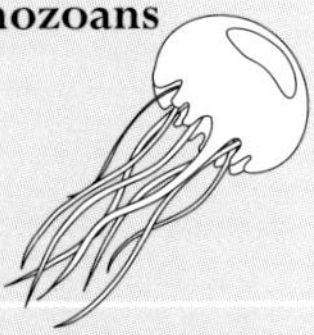

The Echinoderms – sea urchins, starfish, etc.

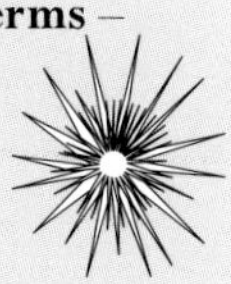

The Fish – rays, sharks, etc.

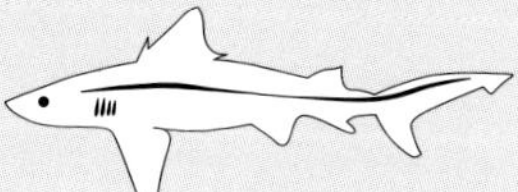

The Seaweeds, Sponges and Corals

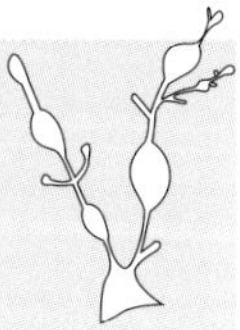

The Polychaetes – true worms.

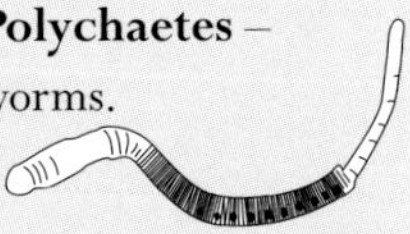

The Angiosperms and Others – flowering and other plants.

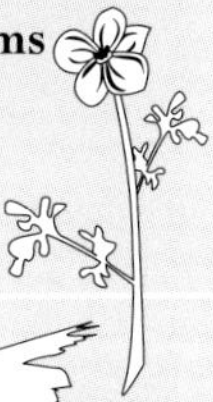

The Birds

The Reptiles and Amphibians

The Mammals

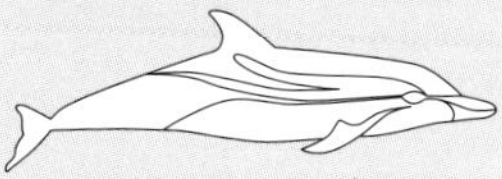

The Insects and Other Invertebrates

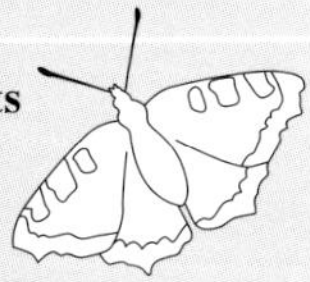

The Sublittoral Zone

In the areas where the ecosystem has not been badly damaged by overfishing or pollution, the sublittoral zone is usually full of life. This is especially true where the sea bed is composed of rocky reefs or shoals, where a wide variety of marine animals and plants take advantage of the shelter from both the oceanic currents and from predators. These include many crustaceans such as shrimps, prawns, crabs and lobsters, as well as starfish, sea urchins, molluscs and the fry of various fish. The rocks themselves are often covered with seaweeds, sponges and sea anemones. Where there is no hard cover, the sea bed is occupied by far fewer organisms. The ones that are able to survive there are almost all burrowing species that live for some or all of their lives under the surface. These include marine worms, certain bivalves, and some of the smaller crustaceans. Many flatfish also partially dig themselves into the sand for camouflage. Above them swim fish of all sizes, as well as turtles, squid, cuttlefish, and also marine mammals such as dolphins, porpoises and whales.

The Food Chain

The plants and animals of a particular habitat, combined with local environmental factors such as climate, together combine to create what is known as an 'ecosystem'. At its simplest, the feeding hierarchy within this can be represented by what is known as a food chain. It charts the flow of nutrients from primary producers such as plants through various levels of consumers to the dominant predators. Such approaches are overly simplistic, however, and are better portrayed as food webs – these are far more detailed, and when constructed accurately, show the often complex interactions between the various organisms in the system. The food chain in the three main zones of the seashore is dominated by mankind's activities; however, at the top of the system there are many natural predators. These can

The food chain is topped by mammals.

be broadly divided into two — those that hunt out of the water, and those that hunt in it. Some species, such as certain birds and mammals like the otter, are included in both groups.

At the lowest level are unicellular algae — they are eaten by various creatures, such as small fish. Some of these are then eaten by larger animals, such as predatory fish or birds. This process goes on until the highest level is reached; this place, in many cases, is taken by mankind.

Evolution

The seashore has borne witness to many of the great evolutionary changes, from when the very first creatures crawled out of the sea and began life on land. Shorelines can be good places to see the remaining evidence, as the exposed rocks found there often contain common fossils such as ammonites, belemnites, and various species of seashells.

Fascinating fossils can often be found on the shoreline.

NAMING AND TAXONOMY

All the documented species of organism have a scientific name that is composed of two main parts. This is called the binomial classification or binomial nomenclature system. Although two-part naming had been in use for some time, it was first properly established by Carolus Linnaeus in the eighteenth century. It has been developed and revised continuously since then. Every named organism fits into a strict hierarchy that runs from the Kingdom (the highest level), through the Phylum, Class, Order, Family, Genus, and finally Species. There are several different naming conventions within this regime, each with its own variations. Alongside the scientific names, many animals and plants also have common names. These should only be used with caution, however, as the same names are often used for different species, depending on which country you are in. As an example, let us examine a simplified version of the classification of the European Lobster, *Homarus gammarus*; it is listed as:

Kingdom: Animalia
Phylum: Arthropoda
Class: Malacostraca
Order: Decapoda
Family: Nephropidae
Genus: Homarus
Species: gammarus (Linnaeus, 1758)

This means that it was described for science by Linnaeus in 1758; that it belongs to the Homarus genus; which belongs to the Nephropidae family (the Clawed lobsters); which in turn are in the Order Decapoda (ten-legged crustaceans); in the Class Malacostraca; the Phylum Arthropoda (arthropods), and the kingdom Animalia (the animals).

SEASHELLS

Mollusca

Alarge number of mollusc species live in the zones encompassed by this book – the empty shells of even more can sometimes be found washed up on the beach. All molluscs are included in the phylum Mollusca – this is a scientific grouping that includes the classes Polyplacophora (chitons), Bivalvia (bivalves), Scaphopoda (tusk shells), Gastropoda (univalves or snails) and Cephalopoda (octopus, squid and cuttlefish). The shelled species range in size from tiny snails of around 2–3 mm to the mighty Giant Clam (*Tridacna gigas*), one museum specimen of which measures 137 cm (54 in) long and weighs 263 kg (580 lb). While most are slow-moving or immobile creatures, others such as the squid are capable of great speeds. Indeed, the biggest mollusc of all is the Colossal Squid (*Mesonychoteuthis hamiltoni*), which it is thought reaches up to 14 metres (46 ft) in length. The vast proportion of molluscs are marine, although they also occur in freshwater and on land. In all, there are around 112,000 species of mollusc, although there may be many more undiscovered in the depths of the oceans.

GASTROPODS

KINGDOM: ANIMALIA PHYLUM: MOLLUSCA
CLASS: GASTROPODA; CUVIER, 1797

Gastropods are a class of molluscs that include land snails and slugs as well as most of the single-shelled 'seashell' species. There are about 70–75,000 species known to man – the figure is not exact because of identification difficulties. Some of the better known ones include cowries and conchs, and all have a spiral twist to their shells known as torsion. They move using a powerful muscular foot, and usually have eyes at the tips of tentacles which project from the head. A lot of gastropods have a trapdoor-like structure called an operculum which they can open and close at will. This is used primarily for defence.

Babylonia zeylanica PERFORATED BABYLON

The Perforated Babylon is also known as the Indian Babylon and the Ivory Shell. It is found on coral reefs in the Indo-Pacific from India to Indonesia and Taiwan. It is a member of the whelk family, and as such is an active carnivore that preys on other molluscs. Typically, these are bivalves such as mussels or clams, which it seizes and then prises open with its large muscular foot before consuming the contents. The eggs are laid in a large capsule, and when these hatch, the larvae, which do not have a swimming stage, are tiny miniatures of the adults, with complete shells, which are able to crawl immediately.

Descriptor: Bruguiere, 1789

Order: Caenogastropoda

Family: Buccinidae

Genus: Babylonia

Species: zeylanica

Distribution: Indo-Pacific, from India across to Indonesia and Taiwan

Size: 50–85 mm (2–3 in)

COMMON WHELK *Buccinum undatum*

Descriptor: Linnaeus, 1758

Order: Caenogastropoda

Family: Buccinidae

Genus: Buccinum

Species: undatum

Distribution: Both sides of northern Atlantic and Mediterranean

Size: 130–160 mm (5–6 in)

Also known as the Waved or Common Northern Whelk, the Common Whelk is a large species that is usually found below the tidal zone, although it sometimes occurs in deep rock pools. It is distributed throughout the cold waters of both coasts of the northern Atlantic, as well as in the Mediterranean Sea. It prefers areas where the sea bed is soft, typically down to about 200 metres (656 ft). It does, however, sometimes go much deeper than this. Common whelks are collected commercially in traps for the food trade.

Calliostoma zizyphinum PAINTED TOP SHELL

The Painted Top Shell, which has a series of red and pink or purple markings, is a small conical species of seashell with a flat base that grows to around 30 mm (1 in) high. There are usually four or five tentacles projected out from the front of the foot – these, and the surrounding tissues, may also be coloured with red and pink. It is commonly found in rocky tidal pools that have a good covering of seaweeds, where it feeds on various small creatures such as hydriods. It lives down to depths of about 300 metres (984 ft) along the coasts of the eastern Atlantic Ocean from the United Kingdom to Morocco.

Descriptor: Linnaeus, 1758

Order: Archaeogastropoda

Family: Calliostomatidae

Genus: Calliostoma

Species: zizyphinum

Distribution: Eastern Atlantic from the United Kingdom to Morocco

Size: 20–32 mm (1–1¼ in)

PACIFIC OR TRUMPET TRITON

Charonia tritonis

The Pacific or Trumpet Triton is sometimes also referred to as the Giant Triton, because it grows to such large sizes – the bigger specimens may reach 600 mm (24 in) in length. They are distributed across the tropical waters of the Indo-West Pacific as well as in some of the warmer temperate regions, down to depths of about 40 metres (131 ft). They are very active predators, and are one of the few creatures that is able to prey on the Crown of Thorns starfish, a major pest of coral reefs. They hunt by smell, and once a potential victim – which may be anything from a mollusc to a sea urchin – has been detected, move in for the kill at full speed. The large muscular foot is used to grasp the prey while the radula – a rasp-like tongue – is used to bore a hole into the soft tissues within.

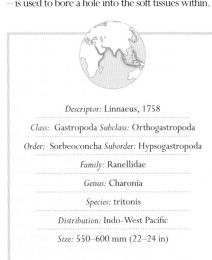

Descriptor: Linnaeus, 1758	
Class: Gastropoda	*Subclass:* Orthogastropoda
Order: Sorbeoconcha	*Suborder:* Hypsogastropoda
Family: Ranellidae	
Genus: Charonia	
Species: tritonis	
Distribution: Indo-West Pacific	
Size: 550–600 mm (22–24 in)	

TIGER COWRY
Cypraea tigris

Found in shallow waters throughout the Indo-Pacific region, from Africa to Hawaii, the Tiger Cowry is often locally abundant. It is typically between 80–100 mm (3–4 in) long, but much larger specimens sometimes occur, especially in the vicinity of the Hawaiian Islands. It lives on rocky ground as well as on reefs, where it feeds by browsing on algae and other sessile organisms such as sponges. During the day, cowries hide under rocks and in crevices; at night they venture out to feed. The shell's markings can be highly variable.

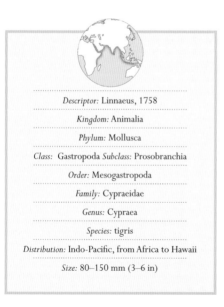

Descriptor: Linnaeus, 1758

Kingdom: Animalia

Phylum: Mollusca

Class: Gastropoda *Subclass:* Prosobranchia

Order: Mesogastropoda

Family: Cypraeidae

Genus: Cypraea

Species: tigris

Distribution: Indo-Pacific, from Africa to Hawaii

Size: 80–150 mm (3–6 in)

TRAPEZIUM HORSE CONCH *Fasciolaria trapezium*

Descriptor: Linnaeus, 1758

Order: Caenogastropoda

Family: Fasciolariidae;
Subfamily: Fasciolariinae

Genus: Fasciolaria

Species: trapezium

Distribution: East African coast
and Indo-West Pacific

Size: 150–250 mm (6–10 in)

Known by a variety of different names, including the Fox's Head and the Striped Fox Horse Conch, the Trapezium Horse Conch is distributed across the Indo-West Pacific region, from the East African coast to Indonesia, but is most common around the Indian sub-continent. It grows to a maximum of about 250 mm (10 in), but is usually somewhat less than this at around 150–175 mm (6–7 in). The markings on the shell can be extremely variable – in the specimen shown here, many of the brown lines have been worn away.

Lambis chiragra CHIRAGRA SPIDER CONCH

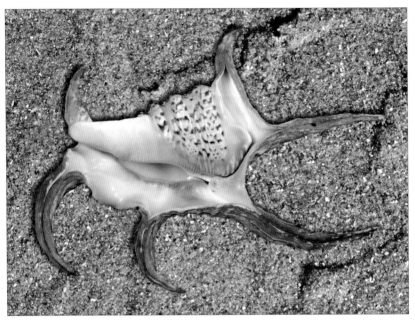

L ike all the spider conches, the Chiragra Spider
Conch has a heavy shell with long, curved arm-like
features. It is a common species throughout its range,
which extends across the eastern Indian Ocean and into
the west Pacific Ocean; it reaches as far as Taiwan in the
north, and Australia in the south. It is a shallow water
reef species that is sometimes found in tidal pools,
and grows to a maximum of 300 mm (12 in). Most
specimens are, however, significantly smaller than this,
typically being 175–200 mm (7–8 in).

Descriptor: Linnaeus, 1758

Order: Caenogastropoda

Family: Strombidae

Genus: Lambis

Species: chiragra

Distribution: Eastern Indian
Ocean and West Pacific, north
to Taiwan, south to Australia

Size: Typically to
175–200 mm (7–8 in)

COMMON SPIDER CONCH *Lambis lambis*

Descriptor: Linnaeus, 1758

Class: Gastropoda

Order: Caenogastropoda

Family: Strombidae

Genus: Lambis

Species: lambis

Distribution: Indo-West Pacific

Size: Typically to 100–125 mm (4–5 in)

Also known as the Smooth Spider Conch, the Common Spider Conch is a locally abundant species that is found in shallow reef areas throughout the Indo-West Pacific region. It is harvested across its range for food, as well as for the decorative qualities of its shell. This grows to a maximum of 200 mm (8 in), but is more typically between 100 and 125 mm (4–5 in). Females have the finger-like projections pointing slightly upwards, whereas those of the male are smaller and flatter.

Lambis scorpius SCORPION SPIDER CONCH

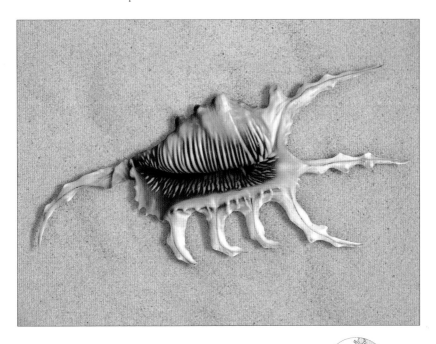

The Scorpion Spider Conch has a distinctive shape, with seven large finger-like projections. It is found in shallow waters of the Indo-Pacific, from Northern Australia to the Philippines. It usually grows to around 160 mm (6 in) in length, with the females being larger than the males. Like the other 65 or so members of the Strombidae family, this species lays its eggs in long strands which are held together by a jelly-like material. While spider conches will browse on algae, they are also voracious carnivores, and will hunt and eat many creatures, especially other molluscs.

Descriptor: Linnaeus, 1758

Class: Gastropoda

Order: Neotaenioglossa

Family: Strombidae

Genus: Lambis

Species: scorpius

Distribution: Northern Australia to the Philippines

Size: 160 mm (6 in)

COMMON PERIWINKLE

Littorina littorea

The Common Periwinkle is found on rocks and in tidal pools on both sides of the northern Atlantic Ocean, where it often abounds. When the tide is out, it secures itself using a moisture-saving mucus in a firm position – often in a shaded place – to await the return of the sea. Once safely underwater, it resumes feeding on algae which it rasps away from hard surfaces using its radula. It usually grows to between 15 and 40 mm (½–1½ in), and has a very variable coloration. The main predators of the Common Periwinkle are sea birds.

Descriptor: Linnaeus, 1758

Class: Gastropoda

Order: Megagastropoda

Family: Littorinidae

Genus: Littorina

Species: littorea

Distribution: Both sides of Northern Atlantic

Size: 15–40 mm (½–1½ in)

FLAT PERIWINKLE *Littorina mariae*

Descriptor: Sacchi & Rastelli, 1966

Family: Littorinidae

Genus: Littorina

Species: mariae

Distribution: North-eastern Atlantic and North Sea from United Kingdom to Scandinavia

Size: To 15 mm (½ in)

The Flat Periwinkle is found along the coasts of the north-eastern Atlantic and North Sea, from the United Kingdom in the south, to Scandinavia in the north. It is a small species, usually around 8 mm (¼ in) or so, but can grow to about 15 mm (½ in) in length. It is commonly found in the tidal zone, on rocks or in pools, and is one of the few species to tolerate the brackish water found in estuaries and marshes. When the tide is out it seals itself with an operculum to keep predators out and moisture in. This is a trapdoor-like structure that is made from a tough chitinous material.

Murex pectin VENUS COMB MUREX

The Venus Comb Murex, which is distributed across the Indo-Pacific region, is equipped with a distinctive array of sharp spines – these are used for defence purposes. It is a predator, particularly on other molluscs, and feeds on them by clamping itself to the victim's shell and then boring a hole through to the soft tissues inside. It will also eat sponges and any other small invertebrates it can catch. These sea snails grow to a maximum size of around 100–150 mm (4–6 in), with the females having longer spines than the males. This species is usually found on reefs or on flat sandy areas.

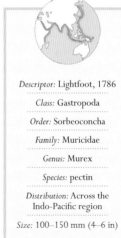

Descriptor: Lightfoot, 1786

Class: Gastropoda

Order: Sorbeoconcha

Family: Muricidae

Genus: Murex

Species: pectin

Distribution: Across the Indo-Pacific region

Size: 100–150 mm (4–6 in)

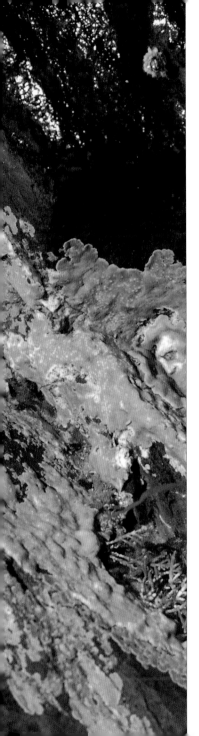

COMMON LIMPET
Patella vulgata

The Common Limpet is found in the intertidal zone attached to rocks along many coasts of the northeastern Atlantic region, from Norway to the Mediterranean. It is not, however, found in the North Sea. It can grow to in excess of 75 mm (3 in) across, and varies in shape depending on the conditions it experiences. In places where the waves are particularly powerful, for instance, the shell tends to be much flatter, as the lower profile helps to reduce wave impact. It is able to hold fast against significant amounts of force due to the powerful clamping pressures which its strong muscular foot can exert. It feeds on marine algae.

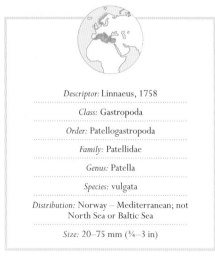

Descriptor: Linnaeus, 1758

Class: Gastropoda

Order: Patellogastropoda

Family: Patellidae

Genus: Patella

Species: vulgata

Distribution: Norway – Mediterranean; not North Sea or Baltic Sea

Size: 20–75 mm (¾–3 in)

REGAL MUREX *Phyllonotus regius*

Descriptor: Swainson, 1821

Order: Sorbeoconcha; *Suborder:* Hypsogastropoda

Family: Muricidae

Genus: Phyllonotus

Species: regius

Distribution: Baja California, Mexico – Peru

Size: 100–140 mm (4–6 in)

Found in shallow waters along the Pacific coast of North and South America, from the Gulf of California to Peru, the Regal Murex is a common species, and grows to a maximum of around 140 mm (6 in) in length. Like the other members of the Murex family, it is a predator on other molluscs as well as on marine worms and barnacles. It is capable of moving relatively quickly, a process it achieves in a series of small jumps. It has a pale to white coloration overall, but is a distinctive pink around the aperture.

Strombus gigas CARIBBEAN QUEEN CONCH

The Caribbean Queen Conch, which is also known by many other names including 'Pink Conch', or simply 'Queen Conch', is distributed across the Neotropical Atlantic waters of the coasts of Florida, southern Mexico, Venezuela, Brazil and the Caribbean. With a maximum length of around 300 mm (12 in), it is the largest mollusc found in North America, and one of only six conch species to occur outside the Indo-Pacific region. Its favoured habitats are large beds of Turtle grass (Thalassia) and Manatee grass (Cymodocea) at depths ranging from 1 to 30 metres (3–98 ft), where it feeds on algae.

Descriptor: Linnaeus, 1758

Order: Sorbeoconcha

Family: Strombidae

Genus: Strombus

Species: gigas

Distribution: Florida and the Caribbean south to Brazil

Size: 250–300 mm (10–12 in); up to 2 kg (4 lb)

PITCHER-SHAPED STROMB *Strombus urceus*

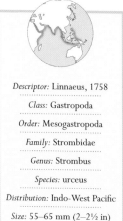

Descriptor: Linnaeus, 1758

Class: Gastropoda

Order: Mesogastropoda

Family: Strombidae

Genus: Strombus

Species: urceus

Distribution: Indo-West Pacific

Size: 55–65 mm (2–2½ in)

Also known as the Scorpion Shell or the Spider Shell, the Pitcher-shaped Stromb is distributed across the Indo-West Pacific region, including the coasts of northern Australia. This species is usually found in low littoral and sublittoral zones to depths of around 40 metres (131 ft) where the sea bed is sandy or muddy. It feeds in groups on various species of algae as well as general detritus. Its coloration and markings can be highly variable.

Tibia insulaechorab ARABIAN TIBIA

The Arabian Tibia belongs to a group that are sometimes referred to as 'shinbone' shells, as per the scientific name of the genus. It is found in the northern parts of the Indian Ocean as well as the Red Sea, in waters down to a depth of about 50 metres (164 ft). It has a long spike, and can reach a maximum length of about 200 mm (8 in), with a variable coloration that can be anywhere from cream to brown. There is a spiral band of a darker brown colour along the leading edge of each whorl.

Descriptor: Röding, 1798

Class: Gastropoda

Order: Caenogastropoda

Family: Strombidae

Genus: Tibia

Species: insulaechorab

Distribution: North Indian Ocean; Red Sea

Size: 120–200 mm (5–8 in)

CHITONS

KINGDOM: ANIMALIA PHYLUM: MOLLUSCA
CLASS: POLYPLACOPHORA; J.E. GRAY, 1821

Chitons, which are sometimes called coat-of-mail shells, belong to the class Polyplacophora. They are occasionally found attached to the underside of rocks in pools. There are around 1,000 different species in the group, all of which are marine. Most live in shallow water, although a few have been discovered at great depths. Their shells are made up of eight plates that fit closely together – these are articulated, so that the shell can be curved to fit closely against a range of different surface shapes. In this manner, it affords a considerable amount of protection.

BIVALVES

KINGDOM: ANIMALIA PHYLUM: MOLLUSCA
CLASS: BIVALVIA; LINNAEUS, 1758

Bivalves are molluscs which usually have two separate parts to their shells – well known examples include mussels, scallops and clams. There are around 30,000 different species, all of which are filter feeders on floating particles or microscopic creatures. Some are found exclusively in freshwater, but the vast majority are marine. There are three basic lifestyles – those that attach themselves to a surface, those that burrow, and those that are capable of swimming freely. These lifestyles vary from species to species.

STRIPED COQUINA CLAM *Donax semistriatus*

Descriptor: Poli, 1795

Class: Bivalvia

Order: Veneroida

Family: Donacidae

Genus: Donax

Species: semistriatus

Distribution: Mediterranean Sea

Size: To 25 mm (1 in)

The Striped Coquina Clam is found in shallow waters of the eastern reaches of the Mediterranean Sea. It has developed a remarkable ability to exploit the movement of water – it will jump into the surf on a rising tide, using its foot and siphons to catch a wave, deliberately allowing itself to be pulled inshore. It can be extremely variable in both shape and coloration, making exact identification very difficult. It is particularly sensitive to the presence of pollutants or large amounts of suspended particles, such as those created by dredging or other construction work. Consequently, it is an important indicator species for ecosystem evaluation.

Glycymeris glycymeris DOG COCKLE

The Dog Cockle is distributed throughout the shallow waters of the North Atlantic region. It lives on sand or shingle down to about 100 metres (328 ft), where it burrows into the sea bed. It feeds on plankton that it filters from the surrounding water. The very nearly circular shell is heavily constructed to protect it from the many predators that live in its habitats. It has a cream, pink or brown coloured background which is in turn marked with an intricate series of red or purple zigzags. The surface is also covered with a large number of short, fine hairs.

Descriptor: Linnaeus, 1758

Class: Bivalvia

Order: Arcoidea

Family: Glycymerididae

Genus: Glycymeris

Species: glycymeris

Distribution: North Atlantic

Size: 40–70 mm (1½–2¾ in)

COMMON OR BLUE MUSSEL

Mytilus edulis

The Common or Blue Mussel is distributed across the northern hemisphere in both temperate and polar waters. The two halves of its dark blue coloured shell fit tightly together – this affords it considerable protection against predators, and allows it to remain out of water for many hours at a time without drying out. It attaches itself to a firm substrate using a very strong thread called a byssus, which is tough enough to ensure that it will not be dislodged by the action of the waves. It also uses these threads to entangle predators such as dog whelks, making it very risky for them to venture into well established mussel beds. These bivalves feed by filtering plankton from the surrounding water.

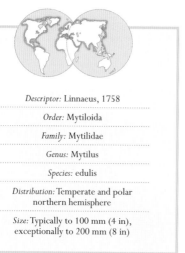

Descriptor: Linnaeus, 1758

Order: Mytiloida

Family: Mytilidae

Genus: Mytilus

Species: edulis

Distribution: Temperate and polar northern hemisphere

Size: Typically to 100 mm (4 in), exceptionally to 200 mm (8 in)

SCALLOPS

KINGDOM: ANIMALIA   PHYLUM: MOLLUSCA
CLASS: BIVALVIA   ORDER: OSTREOIDA   SUBORDER: PECTININA
SUPERFAMILY: PECTINOIDEA   FAMILY: PECTINIDAE

Scallops are bivalves that have the ability to swim freely – this unlikely method of movement is achieved by opening and closing the shells rapidly in a sort of flapping manner. Each time this is done, water is sucked in and then squirted out in a jet using powerful central muscles. Not all scallops exploit this facility, however, and many attach themselves to fixed surfaces with a byssus.

The life-cycle of the scallop is very interesting – these creatures are capable of changing sex, and depending on their gender at the time of reproduction, they either release eggs or sperm into the surrounding water. Any eggs that are successfully fertilized then sink to the sea bed where they remain until the larvae hatch a few weeks later. They then drift with the plankton until they have developed sufficiently to settle on the sea bed and begin growing into adults. This process can take many years.

RAZOR SHELLS

KINGDOM: ANIMALIA PHYLUM: MOLLUSCA

CLASS: BIVALVIA ORDER: VENEROIDA

FAMILY: SOLENIDAE GENUS: ENSIS

Razor shells – also known as 'Jack-knife clams' – are distinctive due to their elongate shells. They are distributed across the northern hemisphere in shallow water along many of the Atlantic and Pacific coasts. They can be found in the lower tidal and upper sublittoral zones where they burrow into sand or coarse mud. When the tide is in, they rise sufficiently for their siphon to reach into the water. Should danger threaten, they burrow further into the sand at an incredible speed. The primary threat is from large creatures such as seabirds like the oystercatcher; however, they are also preyed upon by carnivorous worms. Razor shells are also collected in some areas for fishing bait or human consumption. Where there are extensive colonies of Jack-knife clams, large piles of empty shells often accumulate near the high water mark.

SEA SLUGS

KINGDOM: ANIMALIA   PHYLUM: MOLLUSCA   CLASS: GASTROPODA
ORDER: OPISTHOBRANCHIA   SUBORDER: NUDIBRANCHIA

Nudibranchs – commonly known as sea slugs – are molluscs that over time have dispensed with their protective shells. Some have evolved alternative defences by developing powerful toxins derived from the chemicals contained in the animals they have been feeding on. Such species advertise their unpalatability with bright aposematic warning colours – often these are arranged in spectacular patterns.

Most species of sea slug breathe through feathery gills – these can be quite elaborate, although some respire directly through the skin. There are around 3,000 species known to science, most of which are relatively small; however, the biggest ones can reach as much as 600 mm (24 in) in length.

The majority of sea slugs are predators on small creatures like barnacles, sponges, hydroids and bryozoans. Some, however, are hunters of other sea slugs. They move around using their molluscan muscular foot. Where the currents are particularly strong, many anchor themselves to solid surfaces using powerful glue-like chemicals.

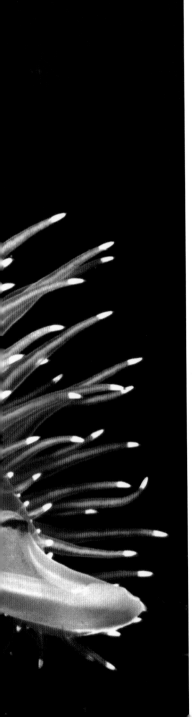

RED-GILLED NUDIBRANCH
Coryphella verrucosa

Found in the shallow waters of the northern Atlantic Ocean, the Red-gilled Nudibranch has, as its name would suggest, a large number of red gills across its back. Each of these long thin structures has a white tip, and the body may be a similar colour, or it may be anywhere from a cream to a yellow-brown. It lives in the littoral and sublittoral zones, on seaweeds and on rocks that are covered with hydroids. It feeds in the open as its colours signal to would-be predators that it is armed with chemical defences. These are derived from the stinging cells of the hydroids it feeds on.

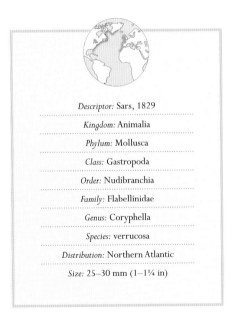

Descriptor: Sars, 1829

Kingdom: Animalia

Phylum: Mollusca

Class: Gastropoda

Order: Nudibranchia

Family: Flabellinidae

Genus: Coryphella

Species: verrucosa

Distribution: Northern Atlantic

Size: 25–30 mm (1–1¼ in)

SPANISH DANCER *Hexabranchus sanguineus*

Descriptor: Ruppell & Leuckart, 1828

Family: Hexabranchidae

Genus: Hexabranchus

Species: sanguineus

Distribution: Tropical Indo-West Pacific

Size: Up to 400 mm (16 in)

The Spanish Dancer is a nudibranch gastropod that is found in the tropical waters of the Indo-Pacific. There are various colour forms – these may be red, yellow or orange – but the mottled form is the most common. It may be seen in a variety of depths, from the littoral down to 200 metres (656 ft) or more. When disturbed or threatened by a predator, it flashes an area of its skin that is coloured a vivid red and white as a warning that it contains toxic chemicals. If this does not work, it usually swims away. This species feeds on a wide variety of sponges and grows to a maximum of about 400 mm (16 in).

Triopha catalinae CLOWN NUDIBRANCH

Also known as the Red-Finger Aeolis, the Clown Nudibranch is distributed from Alaska in the north to Mexico in the south, and from California to Japan. It is sometimes seen in tidal rock pools; however, it is more commonly found in the sublittoral zone down to depths of about 35 metres (115 ft). There is a certain degree of colour variation, with the body ranging from white to light brown, and the tips of the gills can be anything from bright red to pale orange. This creature can reach around 75 mm (3 in) in length, and feeds on various species of bryozoans.

Descriptor: Cooper, 1863

Family: Polyceridae

Genus: Triopha

Species: catalinae

Distribution: Western North America from Alaska to Mexico. Also Japan and South Korea

Size: 60–75 mm (2–3 in)

CEPHALOPODS

KINGDOM: ANIMALIA PHYLUM: MOLLUSCA
CLASS: CEPHALOPODA; CUVIER, 1797

The cephalopods are a fascinating and ancient class within the mollusc order. This group contains the squid, cuttlefish, nautilus and octopus, all of which have very interesting life histories. Although they are closely related to slugs and snails, they have developed tentacles or arms in place of the usual molluscan muscular foot. All the members of this group have excellent dexterity, and are able to manipulate complex objects with their arms.

There are nearly 800 different species of Cephalopod, with the six kinds of nautilus being the only ones to have retained a shell. They are exclusively marine, and in one form or another can be found in all the major seas and oceans of the world, from the shallows to the extreme depths. They have the most highly developed eyes outside the mammal kingdom – consequently, they have superb vision. This helps them seek out and capture prey as well as communicate with each other. They have large brains, and are generally considered to be the most intelligent of all the invertebrates.

CHAMBERED NAUTILUS

Nautilus pompilius

In evolutionary terms, the Nautilus is an ancient genus that belongs to the same class as the squid and cuttlefish. They are nocturnal creatures that swim freely in the waters of the Indian and south-western Pacific Oceans. Although they spend the daylight hours at depths of between 160 and 330 metres (525–1,083 ft), they move towards the surface at night to hunt for prey using their long tentacles. The females spawn once a year, and lay their eggs on rocks in shallow waters. The members of the Nautilus genus live an unusually long time for cephalopods, with their maximum lifespan being around twenty years. After they have died, their highly buoyant shells may be found washed up on beaches many hundreds of miles away from their natural ranges.

Descriptor: Linnaeus, 1758

Class: Cephalopoda

Order: Nautilida

Family: Nautilidae

Genus: Nautilus

Distribution: The Indo-Pacific between the Andaman Sea and Australia

Size: 150–200 mm (6–8 in)

OCTOPUS

KINGDOM: ANIMALIA PHYLUM: MOLLUSCA
CLASS: CEPHALOPODA SUBCLASS: COLEOIDEA
SUPERORDER: OCTOPODIFORMES ORDER: OCTOPODA; LEACH, 1818

The octopus, with its characteristic shape and eight powerful arms, is an easily recognized member of the cephalopod group. There are almost three hundred different species of octopus, nearly all of which are soft-bodied predators of one kind or another. Their lack of any kind of shell or internal skeleton allows them to squeeze through very narrow gaps, an ability they use to good effect when seeking out prey or safe shelter. A few deep water species retain a small internal shell; however, their environment and life history mean they do not have to chase prey or evade capture by squeezing into narrow places. The largest species is probably either the North Pacific Giant Octopus (*Enteroctopus dofleini*), or the Seven-arm Octopus (*Haliphron atlanticus*). Both of these have been documented as weighing around 70 kg (154 lb), but there are many unconfirmed records of much larger specimens.

CUTTLEFISH

KINGDOM: ANIMALIA   PHYLUM: MOLLUSCA
CLASS: CEPHALOPODA   SUBCLASS: COLEOIDEA
SUPERORDER: DECAPODIFORMES   ORDER: SEPIIDA; ZITTEL, 1895

Cuttlefish are, like the other cephalopods, highly intelligent creatures; however, having said that, they are probably best known for the white cuttlebones used in the pet trade to provide calcium for caged birds. This is an internal shell which is all that remains after an individual has died and its body has decomposed. Cuttlefish have eight arms and two tentacles, as well as excellent vision. They hunt either individually or in packs for small marine creatures, such as shrimps, prawns, fish and crustaceans. Cuttlefish, like many other cephalopods, have tens of thousands of special skin cells called chromatophores – these can change colour at will, and at great speed. This facility is used both as an effective camouflage when hunting prey or evading predators, and as a highly advanced communication system. Cuttlefish are eaten by a wide variety of marine predators, including sharks, dolphins and seals, as well as humans.

SQUID

KINGDOM: ANIMALIA PHYLUM: MOLLUSCA

CLASS: CEPHALOPODA SUBCLASS: COLEOIDEA

SUPERORDER: DECAPODIFORMES ORDER: TEUTHIDA; A. NAEF, 1916

Squid, which are voracious marine predators on fish and other small creatures, are found in seas and oceans across the world. They, like their close relations the cuttlefish, have eight arms and two tentacles, as well as excellent vision. Squid move around primarily by use of a structure called the siphon – this is a narrow tube which can be used to generate a high pressure jet of water, enabling extremely rapid movement. When threatened, squid are able to produce a cloud of dark ink from a storage organ called an ink sac – this hides them from view whilst providing an opportunity to escape.

CRUSTACEANS

KINGDOM: ANIMALIA PHYLUM: ARTHROPODA
SUBPHYLUM: CRUSTACEA; BRÜNNICH, 1772

The Crustaceans include many well known animals such as crabs, lobsters, shrimp and prawns, most of which are marine. The group also includes many less obvious creatures as well, though, such as barnacles, fish lice and terrestrial woodlice. There are around 52,000 recorded species, all of which have an exoskeleton of some description.

Since exoskeletons have a fixed size, they have to be cast off regularly in order to allow room for growth. The process of shedding the shell is called moulting or 'ecdysis', and can be a very dangerous time for the individual concerned, as it leaves them dangerously exposed.

Although there is a great diversity of structural form amongst the crustaceans, ranging from immobile barnacles, to parasitic lice, to large crabs, they all share a similar life cycle. This begins when the eggs are fertilized, which happens in a variety of ways, depending on the species. The eggs hatch into first stage larvae called *nauplius* – these then grow until they change to a stage that will grow into the adult form.

ACORN BARNACLES *Chthamalus & Semibalanus species*

Kingdom: Animalia

Phylum: Arthropoda;
Subphylum: Crustacea

Class: Maxillopoda;
Subclass: Thecostraca

Order: Chthamalus &
Semibalanus species

Distribution: Worldwide

Size: To 10 mm (½ in)

Acorn barnacles are small sessile crustaceans that can be found in intertidal zones worldwide. There are a lot of different species – currently about 1,220 are recognized by science. Precise identification is difficult, with even members of different orders being difficult to tell apart without the assistance of an expert. A barnacle begins life as an egg; this hatches into a free swimming larva called a nauplius, which then spends two or three weeks drifting with the plankton. It then metamorphoses into another stage known as a cyprid. It only stays in this form until it finds a suitable solid surface; it then bonds itself to this and changes into a juvenile barnacle. As it develops, it grows six armoured plates around its body, and uses its legs to capture fine food particles from the surrounding water.

Scalpellidae GOOSENECK BARNACLES

Gooseneck Barnacles were once thought to be infant Barnacle Geese; however, they are, in reality, simply stalked crustaceans. They are found in littoral zones throughout the world in temperate and cold waters, attached to rocks and various other solid surfaces. Although most barnacles filter their food from the surrounding water using their feathery feet, these creatures instead rely on the circulation of sea water caused by the action of the waves to bring food directly to them. As a consequence of this, they only live in places where the water is particularly rough. Although most Gooseneck Barnacles only grow to around 75–100 mm (3–4 in), some can reach up to 200 mm (8 in) in length.

Descriptor: Pilsbry, 1916

Subphylum: Crustacea

Class: Cirripedia

Order: Pedunculata

Family: Scalpellidae

Genus: Pollicipes and Lepas

Distribution: Worldwide in temperate and cold waters

Size: 75–200 mm (3–8 in)

SHORE CRAB

Carcinus maenas

The Shore Crab, which is also known as the Green Crab or European Green Crab, is distributed across the cold and temperate waters of the world. It is an extremely invasive species that can be found in large numbers in the littoral zone. Although it is native to European shores, it appears to have been spread by human activity, and in the last two hundred years it has spread to America, South Africa and Australia. It usually has a dark green carapace that may measure up to 90 mm (3½ in) in width and 60 mm (2½ in) in length. There are many colour variations, however, including red, brown and grey forms. It feeds on both plant and animal matter, ranging from carrion to small invertebrates.

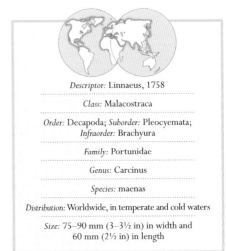

Descriptor: Linnaeus, 1758

Class: Malacostraca

Order: Decapoda; *Suborder:* Pleocyemata; *Infraorder:* Brachyura

Family: Portunidae

Genus: Carcinus

Species: maenas

Distribution: Worldwide, in temperate and cold waters

Size: 75–90 mm (3–3½ in) in width and 60 mm (2½ in) in length

EDIBLE CRAB *Cancer pagurus*

Descriptor: Linnaeus, 1758

Order: Decapoda; *Infraorder:*
Brachyura

Family: Cancridae

Genus: Cancer

Species: pagurus

Distribution: North Atlantic,
North Sea and Mediterranean

Size: Carapace width of
200–250 mm (8–10 in)

The Edible Crab is distributed across the north Atlantic Ocean, as well as the North Sea and the Mediterranean Sea, from Norway to Morocco. It is a heavily built species that is abundant in many places. It usually occurs on rocky ground in the sublittoral zone down to about 100 metres (328 ft), however, small individuals may also sometimes be found in tidal rock pools. They hide in holes and under rocks during the day, coming out to feed at night. They prey on invertebrates such as other crabs, as well as marine worms and molluscs. They can live for up to 20 years, by which time their carapaces will have reached a width of about 250 mm (10 in), and their bodies will weigh around 3 kg (6½ lb).

FIDDLER CRABS

DESCRIPTOR: LEACH, 1814 KINGDOM: ANIMALIA PHYLUM:
ARTHROPODA; SUBPHYLUM: CRUSTACEA CLASS: MALACOSTRACA
ORDER: DECAPODA; INFRAORDER: BRACHYURA
FAMILY: OCYPODIDAE GENUS: UCA
DISTRIBUTION: WEST AFRICA, THE WESTERN ATLANTIC, EASTERN
PACIFIC AND INDO-PACIFIC SIZE: WIDTH 25–50 MM (1–2 IN)

There are about 97 species of fiddler crabs, which are sometimes called calling crabs, all of which are relatively small creatures, reaching a maximum carapace width of about 50 mm (2 in). They are usually found on muddy banks, mangrove swamps, salt marshes or sandy beaches, where they often teem in vast numbers. There is a wide variety of colours, with their carapaces being anywhere from bright blue to dull brown. They are active during the day, and live in burrows that may be up to 60 cm (24 in) deep.

SPIDER CRAB *Maja squinado*

Descriptor: Herbst, 1788

Order: Decapoda; Infraorder: Brachyura

Family: Majidae

Genus: Maja

Species: squinado

Distribution: North-east Atlantic and the Mediterranean

Size: Body to 200 mm (8 in), span of claws to 1.5 m (5 ft)

The Spider Crab is also known as the European Spider Crab, Spiny Spider Crab, or Spinous Spider Crab. It is notable for the enormous span of its legs – up to 1.5 metres (5 ft) in the larger individuals, which would be around eight years old and have carapaces that measure about 200 mm (8 in) in length. It is omnivorous, being a plant feeder on various seaweeds, a scavenger on any carrion it can find, and a predator on molluscs, sea urchins, starfish, marine worms and more or less anything else it can catch. The females can produce eggs up to four times a year – when these hatch they do so as free swimming larvae. This is followed by a bottom-dwelling phase, then development into an adult begins.

Palaemon serratus COMMON PRAWN

Distributed across the Eastern Atlantic, from the United Kingdom to Spain, as well as in the Western Mediterranean, the Common Prawn grows to a maximum body length of about 75 mm (3 in). This species of prawn is largely transparent, although sometimes it may have an underlying green or brown hue. It is marked with a series of thin vertical lines that help to break up its outline. It is commonly found amongst seaweed and under rocks in tidal pools, but also occurs throughout the sublittoral zone to great depths. It feeds on small particles of food that may be either plant or animal in origin.

Descriptor: Pennant, 1777

Order: Decapoda

Family: Palaemonidae

Genus: Palaemon

Species: serratus

Distribution: Eastern Atlantic from United Kingdom to Spain; Western Mediterranean

Size: 50–100 mm (2–4 in)

SQUAT LOBSTERS

KINGDOM: ANIMALIA PHYLUM: ARTHROPODA

SUBPHYLUM: CRUSTACEA CLASS: MALACOSTRACA

ORDER: DECAPODA INFRAORDER: ANOMURA

SUPERFAMILY: GALATHEOIDEA

FAMILY: GALATHEIDAE AND CHIROSTYLIDAE

Squat lobsters, in spite of the name, are not lobsters at all, but are actually more closely related to hermit crabs. They are relatively small creatures, with the larger species usually reaching a maximum length of around 150 mm (6 in). They have short, flattened bodies and long legs, but do not have hard shells. Instead, they protect themselves by finding a suitably sized crevice or a hole under a rock and then squeeze themselves in, leaving only their sharp claws facing the outside world. Once safely ensconced, they wait for suitable prey to settle nearby, and then snatch it with their long claws. In between such meals, they sift through any sand or silt they can reach for any edible matter. As an alternative, they will sometimes steal food from sea anemones.

HERMIT CRABS

KINGDOM: ANIMALIA PHYLUM: ARTHROPODA
SUBPHYLUM: CRUSTACEA CLASS: MALACOSTRACA
ORDER: DECAPODA SUBORDER: PLEOCYEMATA
INFRAORDER: ANOMURA SUPERFAMILY: PAGUROIDEA; LATREILLE, 1802

Hermit crabs are crustaceans that live in discarded
seashells. About five hundred species have been recorded
by science, and these are distributed widely across most of the
world. A few are terrestrial, but the vast majority are marine.
While they co-opt protection by living in old seashells, they
often add to their defences by deliberately placing sea anemones
on the shells they are living in. This can be an effective deterrent
against many predators, such as fish.

CLAWED LOBSTERS

KINGDOM: ANIMALIA PHYLUM: ARTHROPODA

SUBPHYLUM: CRUSTACEA CLASS: MALACOSTRACA

ORDER: DECAPODA INFRAORDER: ASTACIDEA

FAMILY: NEPHROPIDAE; DANA, 1852

The family of Clawed Lobsters — Nephropidae — includes the species of lobsters that are known to humans the world over for their great culinary value. Unlike squat lobsters, these species have heavily armoured shells and large, powerful claws. They usually live on rough ground, anywhere from the tidal zone down to significant depths, where they can find shelter under overhanging rocks. They can, however, also be found in sandy areas if there is sufficient cover.

EUROPEAN LOBSTER
Homarus gammarus

The European lobster is a large clawed lobster. It is solitary, nocturnal and territorial, living in holes or crevices in the sea floor during the day. In the summer, lobsters seek mates, and these migrations are the peak time for lobster fishery. The eggs are then carried by the female for around eleven months, meaning that egg-bearing females may be found throughout the year. The diet of the adult European lobster comprises mostly sea-bottom invertebrates such as crabs, molluscs, sea urchins and starfish, but may also include fish and plants. When moulting, lobsters eat a greater proportion of sea urchins and starfish, as a source of calcium. Feeding is reduced in the winter because of the slower metabolic rate brought on by the lower sea temperatures.

Descriptor: Linnaeus, 1758

Order: Decapoda; *Infraorder:* Astacidea

Family: Nephropidae

Genus: Homarus

Species: gammarus

Distribution: Eastern Atlantic Ocean, from Norway to Morocco

Size: Typically to 500 mm (20 in), exceptionally to 1.25 m (4 ft)

NORWAY LOBSTER
Nephrops norvegicus

The Norway lobster, which is also known as the Dublin Bay prawn or langoustine, is a slim orange-pink lobster found in the north-eastern Atlantic Ocean and North Sea as far north as Iceland and northern Norway, and south to Portugal. It is not common in the Mediterranean, except in the Adriatic Sea. This creature's tail is very muscular, and is frequently eaten, often under the name 'scampi'. Norway lobster is particularly popular in Spain and Portugal where, although being cheaper than the European lobster, it tends to be eaten more on special occasions. Norway lobsters are solitary predators, feeding on other animals such as worms and fish. It is an important species for fisheries, being caught mostly by trawling.

Descriptor: Linnaeus, 1758

Order: Infraorder: Astacidea

Family: Nephropidae

Genus: Nephrops

Species: norvegicus

Distribution: North-eastern Atlantic Ocean and North Sea; Adriatic Sea

Size: To 240 mm (10 in)

CARIBBEAN SPINY LOBSTER

Panulirus argus

A lso known as the Florida spiny lobster, the Caribbean spiny lobster is a member of the genus Panulirus. Like its close relatives such as the Australian, California, and Chinese spiny lobsters, it lacks the large pinching claws of the Maine lobsters. Its only defence are the spines that cover its shell, hence the common name. The Caribbean spiny lobster uses a second pair of antennae in sensory perception. These lobsters have a striped body, brown-grey in colour with yellow spots on the segmented tail. They have compound eyes and can detect orientation, form, light and colour. If startled, they will kick their large abdominal tails rapidly to swim away backwards to safety.

Descriptor: Latreille, 1804

Order: Decapoda; *Infraorder:* Astacidea

Family: Nephropidae

Genus: Panulirus

Species: argus

Distribution: Tropical and subtropical waters of Atlantic Ocean, Caribbean and Gulf of Mexico

Size: To 600 mm (24 in)

SEA SLATER *Ligia oceanica*

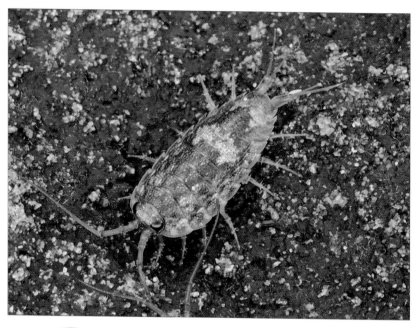

Descriptor: Linnaeus, 1767

Order: Isopoda

Family: Ligiidae

Genus: Ligia

Species: oceanica

Distribution: North-eastern Atlantic and Mediterranean

Size: 20–30 mm (¾–1 in)

The common sea slater is a seashore relative of woodlice that can grow up to 30 mm (1 in) in length. It has a flattened, oval-shaped body that is grey to olive in colour and twice as long as it is broad. It has long antennae, seven pairs of walking legs and two projections at the tip of the abdomen, known as uropods. Its black eyes are very large and obvious, and are similar to the compound eyes found in insects. This species is found in temperate waters from Norway to the Mediterranean Sea and from Cape Cod north to Maine. It is a common species, occurring wherever the substrate of the littoral zone is rocky, and is especially prevalent in crevices and rock pools and under stones. It is a nocturnal omnivore, eating many kinds of seaweed, diatoms and debris.

Talitrus saltator SAND-HOPPER

The sand-hopper is a supralittoral amphipod usually found beneath or amongst debris and decaying algae deposited at the high water mark. During the day it buries itself in the damp sand of the high-tide mark. By being active at night, it avoids both predators and the hot, drying sun. This is an eastern Atlantic species, found around the coast of Britain, the Mediterranean and Northern Europe. It feeds on rotting seaweed in the strandline and navigates using the sun and moon. It can also use horizon level, beach slope, sand moisture and grain size to help orientate itself on the beach. Sand-hoppers escape by jumping erratically if they are disturbed. Reproduction is timed according to the length of the day (photoperiodism) and occurs between late May and August.

Descriptor: Montagu, 1808

Order: Amphipoda; *Suborder:* Gammaridea

Family: Talitridae

Genus: Talitrus

Species: saltator

Distribution: Eastern Atlantic from United Kingdom to Spain; North Sea

Size: 15–20 mm (½–¾ in)

HORSESHOE CRAB
Limulus polyphemus

Often described as a living fossil, the
Horseshoe Crab first evolved in the
Paleaozoic Era around 400 million years ago
and has changed very little since then. It
is actually more closely related to spiders
and scorpions than it is to crabs and other
crustaceans. It is found on the northwestern
Atlantic coasts of North America, especially
in the Gulf of Mexico and the Delaware Bay.
Every spring, these creatures migrate to their
breeding grounds, where the females dig holes
in the sand and lay between 15,000 and 60,000
eggs. When these hatch, the emergent larvae
swim for about a week and then settle, where,
around two weeks later, they then moult into
young crabs. They become mature at around
11 years old, and can live for up to 25 years.

Descriptor:	Linnaeus, 1758
Class:	Merostomata
Order:	Xiphosura
Family:	Limulidae
Genus:	Limulus
Species:	polyphemus
Distribution:	North-western Atlantic coasts
Size:	500 mm (20 in)

SEA ANEMONES & SEA PENS

SEA ANEMONES
KINGDOM: ANIMALIA PHYLUM: CNIDARIA CLASS: ANTHOZOA
SUBCLASS: HEXACORALLIA ORDER: ACTINIARIA

SEA PENS
KINGDOM: ANIMALIA PHYLUM: CNIDARIA CLASS: ANTHOZOA
SUBCLASS: ALCYONARIA ORDER: PENNATULACEA

Sea Anemones and Sea Pens both belong to the Class Anthozoa – this is a grouping that also contains the corals. All the members of this class have specialized stinging cells called nematocysts which they use to help capture prey of various sizes. Sea anemones have these stinging cells arranged on the ends of their tentacles, and should any suitable prey species venture near, they will quickly envelope it. The poisons delivered by the nematocysts are neurotoxic, and they usually paralyse the victim quite quickly. In this manner, they are able to catch animals that are relatively large in comparison to their own size, such as prawns and small fish. They will also consume any small particles that they sieve from the surrounding water.

BEADLET ANEMONE
Actinia equina

The Beadlet Anemone is found attached to hard substrata, both in exposed and sheltered situations, from the upper to lower shore and rarely in subtidal areas to depths of around 20 metres (66 ft). It is highly adapted to the intertidal zone as it tolerates high temperatures and desiccation. This species is also found in estuaries. The Beadlet Anemone has a broad base, which is moderately or firmly adhesive, with a smooth column. It has up to 192 tentacles arranged into six circles. The tentacles readily retract if the animal is disturbed. *Actinia equina* is uniform in colour, with no pattern on the disc, and can be red, brown, green or orange in colour. Bright blue wart-like spots, called acrorhagi, are often found around the inside of the top margin of the column.

Descriptor: Linnaeus, 1758

Order: Actiniaria; *Suborder:* Nynantheae

Family: Actiniidae

Genus: Actinia

Species: equina

Distribution: Eastern Atlantic from Russia to Africa and the Mediterranean

Size: Body to 50 mm (2 in), tentacles to 75 mm (3 in)

SNAKELOCKS ANEMONE

Anemonia viridis

The Snakelocks Anemone is distributed across the north-eastern Atlantic Ocean and the North Sea as well as the Mediterranean Sea. It is found in tidal rock pools in the mid- to lower littoral zone, where it can grow to 50 mm (2 in) in height, with up to 200 tentacles that can be as much as 150 mm (6 in) long. These are usually green – with the colours varying from vivid to muted; the tips of the tentacles are generally pink or purple. The overall coloration is due to large numbers of algae that live within the anemone's tissues; since these are photosynthetic, the species usually chooses to locate itself in a sunny position.

Descriptor: Forskal, 1775

Class: Anthozoa; *Subclass:* Hexacorallia

Order: Actiniaria; *Suborder:* Nynantheae

Family: Actiniidae

Genus: Anemonia

Species: viridis

Distribution: North-eastern Atlantic Ocean and North Sea; Mediterranean

Size: Body to 50 mm (2 in), tentacles to 150 mm (6 in)

STRAWBERRY ANEMONE *Corynactis californica*

Descriptor: Carlgren, 1936

Class: Anthozoa

Order: Corallimorpharia

Family: Corallimorphidae

Genus: Corynactis

Species: californica

Distribution: West coast of United States

Size: 20 cm (8 in)

The Strawberry or Club-tipped Anemone is a colonial species that is found in shady places along the west coast of the United States, from British Columbia in the north, to San Diego in the south. It grows to around 10 cm (4 in) in diameter and 20 cm (8 in) in height, with the tentacles reaching to about 25 mm (1 in) across. It is not a true sea anemone, but is instead a member of the Corallimorphidae family. The members of this group have tentacles with club-shaped tips – these are armed with powerful stinging cells that are used to catch small marine creatures such as those found in the plankton. Corallimorphs are also very similar to corals in some other characteristics, but lack the hard coral skeleton.

SEA PENS

KINGDOM: ANIMALIA PHYLUM: CNIDARIA CLASS: ANTHOZOA
SUBCLASS: ALCYONARIA ORDER: PENNATULACEA; VERRILL, 1865

Sea Pens are anthozoans, and so are in the same class as sea anemones and corals; their order – the Pennatulacea – is extensive with 14 distinct families. They are found in most seas and oceans across the temperate and tropical parts of the world, and are often brightly coloured. While they look like plants with anchored bases, they can, in fact, 'uproot' themselves and relocate, should they feel the need. They can grow to heights of around two metres (6½ ft), and although some species can be found in waters of only 10 metres (33 ft) or so, many live at depths of in excess of 2,000 metres (6,561 ft).

JELLYFISH

KINGDOM: ANIMALIA PHYLUM: CNIDARIA
CLASS: SCYPHOZOA; GOETTE, 1887 ORDERS: STAUROMEDUSAE,
CORONATAE, SEMAEOSTOMEAE AND RHIZOSTOMAE

Jellyfish, which belong to the class Scyphozoa, were among the first multicellular animals to evolve, several hundred million years ago. They quickly established an ecological niche for themselves, and have changed little since then. For such an ancient grouping, there are relatively few species — only 200 or so. They are, however, exceptionally numerous, and are one of the most common sea creatures in the world. The smallest ones are less than a centimetre (½ in) long, with the largest having tentacles that can reach over 40 metres (131 ft) and bodies that may be over two metres (6½ ft) in diameter. The body of an adult jellyfish is composed of up to 98% water — most of the rest is made up of a special jelly that is held between two membranous layers. This is made possible because they do not have any hard structures such as a head or a skeleton. Few jellyfish are able to control where they travel — most are completely tied to the vagaries of the wind and tide, drifting where nature's elements take them. They feed on small fish, crustaceans and plankton.

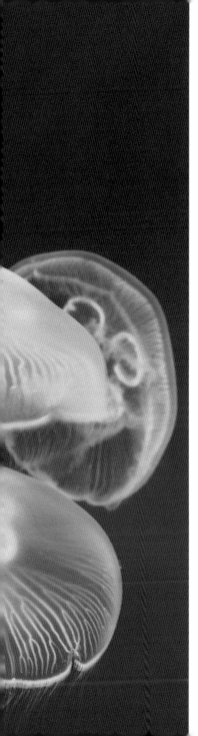

MOON JELLY

Aurelia aurita

Also known as the Saucer Jelly and Common Sea Jelly, the Moon Jelly is distributed throughout the warmer parts of the Atlantic, Indian and Pacific Oceans. It often occurs in huge numbers, and may be found near coasts as well as in brackish water with a very low salt content. Moon Jellies grow to anywhere between 50 mm (2 in) and 400 mm (16 in), and swim by pulsing their bells up and down; this is more to keep them near the surface than it is to move in any particular direction. These jellyfish have extensive tentacles which are used to catch small prey – this includes most of the planktonic species, such as molluscs, fish and crustacean larvae.

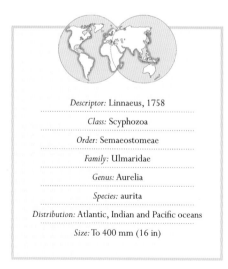

Descriptor: Linnaeus, 1758

Class: Scyphozoa

Order: Semaeostomeae

Family: Ulmaridae

Genus: Aurelia

Species: aurita

Distribution: Atlantic, Indian and Pacific oceans

Size: To 400 mm (16 in)

PURPLE-STRIPED JELLY *Chrysaora colorata*

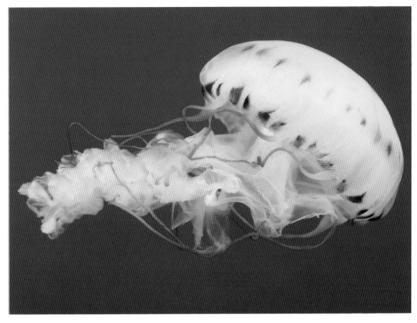

Descriptor: Russell, 1964

Order: Semaeostomeae

Family: Pelagiidae

Genus: Chrysaora

Species: colorata

Distribution: Atlantic and Pacific Oceans and the Mediterranean

Size: Bell diameter to 700 mm (28 in)

The Purple-striped Jelly is distributed across the Atlantic and Pacific Oceans, as well as the Mediterranean Sea, and usually only occurs in small numbers. The bell of this species can grow up to 700 mm (28 in) in diameter and this, as the name would suggest, is generally marked with purple stripes, except in the juveniles. The Purple-striped Jelly has four oral arms and eight tentacles which are equipped with powerful stinging cells; these are strong enough to hurt a human quite painfully. This species preys on small planktonic creatures, such as mollusc, fish and crustacean larvae as well as eggs and copepods.

Chrysaora quinquecirrha STINGING SEA NETTLE

O ften seen in estuaries, the Stinging Sea Nettle is distributed across the Atlantic, Indian and Pacific Oceans. It has a brown bell that can grow to around 250 mm (10 in) in diameter. It has long tentacles which are armed with toxic stinging cells – these can be very painful to a human, but are not life-threatening unless there is an allergy complication. Some of the cells produce a sticky substance rather than a poison, which is used to entrap prey so that it can be manoeuvred into a position ready for consumption. It feeds on a variety of marine creatures from plankton to crustaceans, and even other species of jellyfish.

Descriptor: Desor, 1848

Order: Semaeostomeae

Family: Pelagiidae

Genus: Chrysaora

Species: quinquecirrha

Distribution: Atlantic, Indian and Pacific Oceans

Size: Bell diameter to 250 mm (10 in)

MAUVE STINGER OR PURPLE JELLYFISH

Pelagia noctiluca

The Mauve Stinger or Purple Jellyfish is distributed across the seas and oceans of the warmer parts of the world. It lives at the surface, and maintains its position there by pulsing its bell rhythmically. It is, however, unable to move in any particular direction, and so is at the mercy of the currents. It is primitive, consisting of a simple net composed of naked and largely non-polar neurons. In addition, this species also lacks a gaseous exchange, excretory and circulatory system. These jellyfish often congregate in large swarms, and when caught by the wind, these can easily end up on the shore in huge numbers. It is capable of producing flashes of light, and as a result is sometimes called the 'Nightlight Jellyfish'.

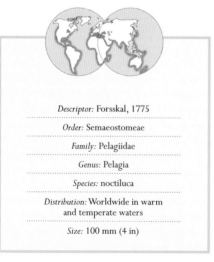

Descriptor: Forsskal, 1775

Order: Semaeostomeae

Family: Pelagiidae

Genus: Pelagia

Species: noctiluca

Distribution: Worldwide in warm and temperate waters

Size: 100 mm (4 in)

ECHINODERMS

KINGDOM: ANIMALIA PHYLUM: ECHINODERMATA

The Echinoderms that are found today are a large, ancient group which arose at the start of the Cambrian period, about 530 million years ago. There are about 7,000 species in total, including the starfish (sea stars), sea urchins, crinoids, sea cucumbers and brittle stars. Their skeletons fossilize well, so there is a good palaeontological record, and it is known that over the eons, many other types also arose, but these have since become extinct. Echinoderms are exclusively marine, and they can be found in all the world's seas and oceans from tidal rock pools to the darkest depths.

All the animals in this phylum have bodies that are radially symmetrical. Their nervous systems are incredibly simple, with none having distinct brains. A by-product of this simplicity is their remarkable ability to regenerate themselves if they are cut into pieces – a single starfish leg, for instance, is capable of growing into a fully functioning individual. Most have separate sexes, and at breeding time the males release clouds of sperm into the water, while the females eject eggs in vast numbers – fertilization is a chance affair.

STARFISH

KINGDOM: ANIMALIA PHYLUM: ECHINODERMATA
CLASS: ASTEROIDEA ORDERS: BRISINGIDA, FORCIPULATIDA,
PAXILLOSIDA, NOTOMYOTIDA, SPINULOSIDA, VALVATIDA AND VELATIDA

Starfish – also known as sea stars – are members of the class Asteroidea. These have a central body with, most commonly, five radial arms. There are around 1,800 different species of starfish, which are all exclusively marine. They can be found all around the world, from the tidal zone into the lowest reaches of the deep sea in a wide variety of habitats. These include coral reefs, tidal rock pools, and kelp forests. Some feed on coral polyps, others on decaying plant or animal matter. Most though, will attack and eat more or less any creature they can subdue.

Asterina gibbosa CUSHION STARFISH

The Cushion Starfish is found along the coasts of the Atlantic Ocean, where it can sometimes be found under rocks or hiding amongst seaweeds in tidal pools. It has five very short arms and grows to about 50 mm (2 in) in diameter. It can be quite variable in colour – ranging from a pale green to a red-brown or orange-yellow. The Cushion Starfish is a very slow moving species that is only capable of travelling at about 25 mm (1 in) per minute. Although it is commonly found on the seashore, it also occurs to depths of around 130 metres (426 ft). These small starfish begin life as males, and then when they are about four years old, they change into females.

Descriptor: Pennant, 1777

Class: Asteroidea

Order: Spinulosida;
Suborder: Leptognathina

Family: Asterinidae

Genus: Asterina

Species: gibbosa

Distribution: Atlantic Ocean

Size: 50 mm (2 in)

COMMON STARFISH *Asterias rubens*

Descriptor: Linnaeus, 1758

Order: Forcipulatida

Family: Asteriidae

Genus: Asterias

Species: rubens

Distribution: Atlantic Ocean and Mediterranean

Size: Typically to 300 mm (12 in), exceptionally to 500 mm (20 in)

As its name would suggest, the Common Starfish is a common species that is found on most of the coasts around the Atlantic Ocean. It also occurs in the Mediterranean Sea, although it is less frequently seen there. It is only found within about 400 metres (1,312 ft) of the shoreline, and sometimes lives in estuarine habitats. At times, it undergoes population booms, and huge numbers congregate. It is a predator on a variety of marine creatures, including molluscs – especially mussels and barnacles, as well as marine worms, crustaceans and other echinoderms. Although it normally grows to about 300 mm (12 in) in diameter, it sometimes reaches 500 mm (20 in), and is usually an orange, brown or red colour.

Astropecten irregularis SAND STAR

The Sand Star is distributed along the coasts of the eastern Atlantic, from Scandinavia in the north to South Africa in the south. It lives below the surface of sand or fine gravel anywhere from the upper sublittoral zone to depths of about 1000 metres (9,842 ft), but is sometimes washed ashore after large storms. It can reach 200 mm (8 in) in diameter, and usually has a sand-coloured or brown body with five short, stiff arms. There is a row of small spines along the edges of each arm, and the underside is a pale white or light brown colour.

Descriptor: Pennant, 1777

Order: Phanerozonia

Family: Astropectinidae

Genus: Astropecten

Species: irregularis

Distribution: Eastern Atlantic, from Scandinavia to South Africa

Size: To 200 mm (8 in)

COMMON SUN STAR *Crossaster papposus*

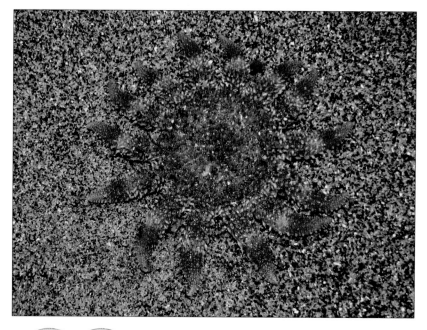

Descriptor: Linnaeus, 1767

Order: Spinulosida;
Suborder: Eugnathina

Family: Solasteridae

Genus: Crossaster

Species: papposus

Distribution: North Atlantic and Pacific Coasts

Size: To 340 mm (13 in)

The Common Sun Star is found along the coasts of the north Atlantic and Pacific Oceans from Alaska and Norway in the north to Maine and Portugal in the south. This species is unusual in that it has more arms than a typical starfish – anywhere from eight to 14 may be seen, as opposed to the more normal average number of five. The upper surface is typically red and covered in lots of small spines; it can grow to a maximum of 340 mm (13 in), although 250 mm (10 in) is more common. It occurs on rocky ground in the sublittoral zone from 10 metres (33 ft) or so down to depths of about 50 metres (164 ft).

Echinaster sepositus RED STARFISH

The Red Starfish is found along the coasts of the eastern Atlantic from the southern side of the English Channel down to the Mediterranean Sea. In this region it is a very common species on rocky shores and amongst eel grass beds, as well as in the sublittoral zone down to about 200 metres (656 ft). It has five well defined arms, a bright red coloration, and grows to a maximum of around 200 mm (8 in). One characteristic feature is that its skin has a soapy texture. It is a predator on various marine creatures, especially barnacles and molluscs.

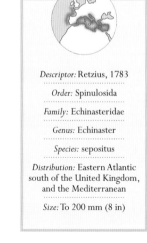

Descriptor: Retzius, 1783

Order: Spinulosida

Family: Echinasteridae

Genus: Echinaster

Species: sepositus

Distribution: Eastern Atlantic south of the United Kingdom, and the Mediterranean

Size: To 200 mm (8 in)

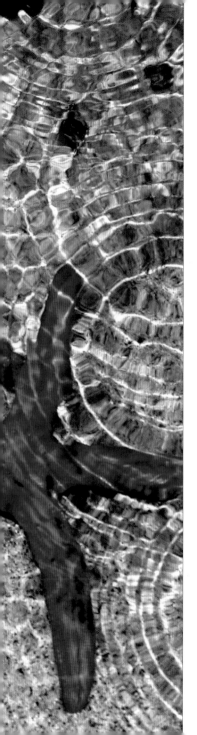

BLUE SEA STAR

Linckia laevigata

Also sometimes called the 'Blue Linckia', the Blue Sea Star is distributed across the tropical Indo-Pacific. It is a common species that is found in shallow waters, especially on reefs and where sea grass abounds, from the lower littoral to the sublittoral zones. It can reach 300 mm (12 in) in diameter, and is more than capable of regrowing any limbs that have been lost. This is often the result of attacks by predators such as pufferfish, large molluscs – especially tritons – and various crustaceans. It feeds on algal films as well as sea bed detritus. In some areas, it has been collected for sale as trinkets to such an extent that it is in serious decline.

Descriptor: Linnaeus, 1758

Class: Asteroidea

Order: Valvatida

Family: Ophidiasteridae

Genus: Linckia

Species: laevigata

Distribution: The tropical Indo-Pacific

Size: To 300 mm (12 in)

OCHRE OR PURPLE SEA STAR

Pisaster ochraceus

The Ochre or Purple Sea Star is found along the Pacific coast of North America from Alaska to California. It is an easily recognized and common species that can vary in colour from orange to purple. It may grow to 400 mm (16 in) in diameter, and has extremely flexible arms which are used to good effect when hunting. It identifies a suitable victim – often a California Mussel – and then engulfs it within its arms. Hydraulic pressure is then used to pry the two halves of the shell apart; once this has been achieved, the Purple Sea Star consumes the hapless prey's soft tissues. Where molluscs are not available, this species will also prey on anything from crabs to barnacles.

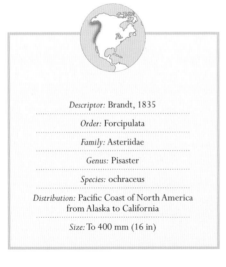

Descriptor: Brandt, 1835

Order: Forcipulata

Family: Asteriidae

Genus: Pisaster

Species: ochraceus

Distribution: Pacific Coast of North America from Alaska to California

Size: To 400 mm (16 in)

BRITTLE STARS

KINGDOM: ANIMALIA PHYLUM: ECHINODERMATA
CLASS: OPHIUROIDEA; GRAY, 1840s

Brittle stars may look like starfish with long, thin, flexible arms, but they are, in fact, members of a completely distinct, but closely related, class of echinoderms. They are exclusively marine, and a large proportion of the nearly 2,000 species are only found in deep water. They are distributed across the world, where they live by filter feeding, scavenging, feeding off decaying animal and plant matter, or predating on small creatures such as shrimps or marine worms. Those species which live in shallow water tend to hide under rocks during the day, and only emerge at night to feed. Unlike starfish, brittle stars use their arms as their main means of moving around. When a food particle is found, it is picked up by the tube feet and moved from one to another until it reaches the mouth, whereupon it is consumed. The largest brittle stars may reach 600 mm (24 in) in diameter, and some species from the deep sea have luminous arms.

SEA URCHINS

KINGDOM: ANIMALIA PHYLUM: ECHINODERMATA
CLASS: ECHINOIDEA; LESKE, 1778

Although sea urchins are closely related to starfish and brittle stars, they do not have any arms. Instead, they have a hard globular shell which is known as a 'test'. This is covered with very sharp spines, and in many species these contain venomous chemicals. This protection is very effective; however, in spite of this, they are still preyed upon by a number of animals. These include crabs, fish – especially wolf eels, sea otters, certain starfish and molluscs, birds, and humans. There are around 700 different species of sea urchin which are distributed worldwide from tidal rock pools to the furthest depths of the deep sea. The largest species is found in the Pacific Ocean – this is called the Red Sea Urchin (*Strongylocentrotus franciscanus*), and it can grow to a test size of nearly 20 cm (8 in). Others have smaller shells, but much longer spines. Since they are only capable of moving slowly on their tube feet, they are not able to hunt down fast-moving prey. Their omnivorous diet is therefore primarily based on fixed or slow-moving organisms, such as seaweed, algae, sponges, barnacles and molluscs. They will also scavenge on any dead creatures that they come across.

SEA CUCUMBERS

KINGDOM: ANIMALIA PHYLUM: ECHINODERMATA
CLASS: HOLOTHUROIDEA

While sea cucumbers are in the same phylum grouping as starfish and sea urchins, they look nothing like them. These strange creatures, which are so named because they have similar proportions to a cucumber, can be found in seas and oceans the world over from tidal shallows to the deep sea. They are exclusively marine, usually nocturnal, and have a series of tentacles – up to 30, arranged around the mouth. Most feed by scavenging on sea bed detritus as well as plankton, and move around using small tube feet. Many species live in holes in the sea bed that they have excavated by burrowing.

FEATHER-STARS

KINGDOM: ANIMALIA PHYLUM: ECHINODERMATA
CLASS: CRINOIDEA; MILLER, 1821

Feather-stars – which are also referred to as crinoids or sea lilies – live in marine environments all over the world, from the sublittoral zone to the depths of the oceans. These days there are around 600 species of these strange creatures, which first evolved during the Ordovician period, some 450 million years ago. At first sight, feather-stars appear to be plants, with a stem off which a number of branches grow. In reality, they are animals which are composed of a stem, a calyx, and a number of arms. They are capable of 'uprooting' themselves and swimming or crawling to a fresh location at will.

FISH

KINGDOM: ANIMALIA PHYLUM: CHORDATA

Fish make up an enormously important part of the marine fauna; however, it is worth noting that there are many entirely different groups of creatures that come under the generic title 'fish'. They do have many common features, though – for a start, they are all cold-blooded, have backbones and are aquatic. While some live in fresh water, the vast majority are exclusively marine – a few are able to live in both environments. Most derive oxygen from the surrounding water through gills, move with two pairs of paired fins, and have dorsal as well as tail fins. Although they typically have scales on their skin, some – for example, eels – do not. Others, such as cartilaginous fish including rays and sharks, have a very tough skin in place of scales. The speed at which fish can swim varies dramatically, with seaweed dwellers such as sea horses being very slow, gentle swimmers. At the other end of the spectrum there are open ocean species like barracuda which can move very rapidly indeed. The range of sizes among fish is also incredible, ranging from a few millimetres in some species to enormous creatures like the whale shark, which grows to at least 16 m (51 ft).

FLATFISH

KINGDOM: ANIMALIA PHYLUM: CHORDATA
CLASS: ACTINOPTERYGII ORDER: PLEURONECTIFORMES

Flatfish make up an interesting group that contains many economically important species including plaice, turbot, megrim, flounder, sole and halibut. There are around 400 in total, and they can be found distributed throughout the world's seas and oceans. Although they are marine, some, such as the flounder, spend the early parts of their lives in the upper reaches of estuaries where the water is effectively entirely fresh. Most flatfish have an upper and a lower side. The upper side is usually cryptically coloured so that when they are lying on the sea bed, they are hidden from predators. Many part-bury themselves too, which provides further camouflage.

Dasyatis kuhlii BLUE-SPOTTED STINGRAY

The Blue-spotted Stingray – also known as the Blue-spotted Ribbontail Ray or Kuhl's Stingray – is covered with characteristic blue spots over a green, grey or brown background coloration. It can grow to a body size of 400 mm (16 in) and an overall length of 700 mm (28 in). It is found in shallow waters across the tropical Indo-West Pacific, where it often buries itself in the sand so that only its eyes are visible. It is commonly seen in estuaries, where it hunts for crabs, shrimps, prawns and molluscs. Any food it captures is crushed in its powerful mouth, which is equipped with special tough plates. Like most stingrays, the tail of this species is equipped with a pair of venomous spines.

Descriptor: Müller & Henle, 1841

Order: Rajiformes

Family: Dasyatidae

Genus: Dasyatis

Species: kuhlii

Distribution: Tropical Indo-West Pacific

Size: Body length to 700 mm (28 in)

COMMON STINGRAY *Dasyatis pastinaca*

Descriptor: Linnaeus, 1758

Order: Rajiformes

Family: Dasyatidae

Genus: Dasyatis

Species: pastinaca

Distribution: Eastern Atlantic, English Channel, Mediterranean, Black Sea, west Baltic

Size: Length to 2.5 m (8 ft)

The Common Stingray is distributed across the eastern Atlantic Ocean, as well as in parts of the English Channel, Mediterranean Sea, Black Sea and the western Baltic. It is found in shallow waters, where it is a bottom feeder that often hides beneath a layer of sand or silt, with only its eyes showing through. It preys on a wide variety of marine creatures, including crabs, molluscs and fish, but will also take carrion – it has powerful jaws that can break through thick shells. If threatened by a large predator, the stingray will attempt to protect itself using the venomous spine at the base of its tail.

Lipophrys pholis COMMON BLENNY

Known by many different names, including Smooth Blenny, Shanny, Mordocet and Clunny, the Common Blenny is a common seashore fish. It can be found in the littoral zone along both the western and eastern coasts of the Atlantic Ocean. When the tide is out, it hides in rock pools or under thick clumps of seaweed – unusually, it does not need to remain in water as it can breathe air. When the tide returns, it ventures forth and hunts for small invertebrates such as amphipods and small molluscs, but will also feed on barnacles and algae.

Descriptor: Linnaeus, 1758

Class: Osteichthyes

Order: Perciformes

Family: Blennidae

Genus: Lipophrys

Species: pholis

Distribution: Atlantic coasts of North America and Europe

Size: 165 mm (6½ in)

LESSER-SPOTTED DOGFISH

Scyliorhinus canicula

Also known as the Small Spotted Catshark, the Lesser-spotted Dogfish is a common cartilaginous fish of the Atlantic Ocean. On the North American side it is found from Canada in the north to Brazil in the south. On the European side, it occurs from Scandinavia down to parts of West Africa. It usually lives on the sea bed of shallow waters where there is rough or muddy ground, feeding on a variety of marine animals, including crabs, fish, molluscs and worms as well as carrion. Adults grow to a maximum of about one metre (3 ft) in length, and have a very rough skin.

Descriptor: Linnaeus, 1758

Class: Elasmobranchii

Order: Carcharhiniformes

Family: Scyliorhinidae

Genus: Scyliorhinus

Species: canicula

Distribution: Atlantic; East: from Scandinavia to West Africa. West: Canada to Brazil

Size: Up to 1 metre (3 ft)

SEAHORSES

KINGDOM: ANIMALIA PHYLUM: CHORDATA
CLASS: ACTINOPTERYGII ORDER: SYNGNATHIFORMES
FAMILY: SYNGNATHIDAE GENUS: HIPPOCAMPUS; CUVIER (1816)

Seahorses are a group of small fish with extremely unusual physical forms and life histories. They belong to the genus Hippocampus, and can be found in both tropical and the warmer temperate seas of the world. They are mostly small creatures, ranging from around 15 mm (½ in) up to about 350 mm (14 in). Since they are very slow-moving, they rely almost entirely on cryptic colours, shapes and patterns to avoid predators, rather than any physical ability to move away from trouble. Some are almost transparent, which makes them even harder to see. They usually hide amongst thick seaweed or in rocky crevices, where they quietly feed on small invertebrates, such as small crustaceans and fish fry. Seahorses are perhaps best known for their unusual breeding habits. After a couple has paired following elaborate courtship rituals, the male fertilizes the female's eggs by releasing sperm into the water around the female. She then lays her eggs into a brood pouch on the male. He gestates them for two to three weeks, after which time they hatch into minute larvae. These either swim freely with the plankton, or settle on the sea bed to develop.

SEAWEEDS, SPONGES & CORALLINES

While most algae are unicellular and microscopic, seaweeds are large, multicellular organisms that dominate the marine environment in many places. There is some debate as to whether seaweeds are true plants or not – either way, they are marine macroalgae, and can be divided into three categories – green, red and brown. Green seaweeds, of which there are around 1,200 species, get their colouring from the fact that they use chlorophyll to photosynthesize. They form an important part of the diets of many marine creatures. There are at least 6,500 species of red algae in the class Rhodophyceae, although because identification is extremely complex, no-one is sure just how numerous the class is. Although the corallines do not look like red algae, they are, in fact, members of this group. The class Phaeophyceae, of which there are about 2,200 species, is made up of brown algae, many of which are commonly known as kelp. These are the largest seaweeds in the world, and some species can reach lengths of up to 60 metres (200 ft).

KNOTTED OR EGG WRACK *Ascophyllum nodosum*

Descriptor: Le Jolis, 1863

Order: Fucales

Family: Fucaceae

Genus: Ascophyllum

Species: nodosum

Distribution: Northern
Atlantic Ocean

Size: Up to 2 metres (6½ ft)

Knotted or Egg Wrack is a common brown algal seaweed that is found in the mid-littoral zone along the northern coasts of the Atlantic Ocean, on both the American and European sides. It is a slow-growing species that has long fronds – up to 2 metres (6½ ft) long, which feature large air sacs. This species can live for many decades, and is often seen on rocky shores where there is some degree of shelter from the waves. In these places, it can be the predominant seaweed. There are several different varieties, and exact identification can be problematic.

Fucus vesiculosus BLADDER WRACK

The Bladder Wrack (also known by many other names including 'rockweed') is a common seaweed that can be found on seashores across the northern hemisphere. It can grow to over 1 metre (3 ft) long, and although the species is very variable, it is easily distinguished by the large numbers of flotation bladders or 'vesicles' which occur in pairs along the fronds. It is often found washed up on the shore in large quantities, especially after stormy weather. It is collected and eaten as a foodstuff in Japan, and across other parts of the world it is harvested and used in many forms for medicinal purposes due to its unusually high iodine content.

Descriptor: Linnaeus, 1753

Class: Phaeophyceae

Order: Fucales

Family: Fucaceae

Genus: Fucus

Distribution: Coasts of Atlantic and Pacific Oceans, North Sea, & western Baltic Sea

Size: 1 metre upwards (3 ft+)

SPONGE SEAWEED *Codium tomentosum*

Descriptor: Stackhouse, 1797

Class: Chlorophyceae

Order: Bryopsidales

Family: Codiaceae

Genus: Codium

Species: tomentosum

Distribution: Atlantic, Indian and Pacific Oceans

Size: 300 mm (12 in)

The Sponge Seaweed – also known as the Velvet Horn – is a common green algal seaweed that is distributed along the coasts of the Atlantic, Indian and Pacific Oceans. It is not tolerant of pollution, and in some parts of its range it is declining for this reason. It is a small plant that is found in the lower littoral zone on rocks and in tidal pools, where it grows from a fixed attachment point. The fronds have a round section, and these branch into two – as the names would suggest, they have a spongy feel with a velveteen texture.

Enteromorpha intestinalis GUT WEED

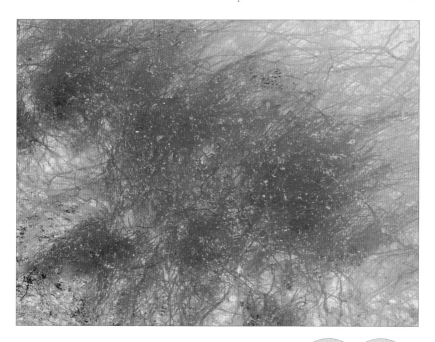

A common green algal seaweed that is distributed along the coasts of the Atlantic, Indian and Pacific Oceans, from the Arctic to the Antarctic. It can be found from the high tide mark down to the sublittoral to a depth of about 7 metres (30 ft) along beaches, estuaries and mangrove swamps. It has air pockets disposed along the fronds to help keep it off the sea bed, and is capable of surviving widely differing salinity levels. Consequently, it is often seen in tidal pools that are only covered by the very highest tides.

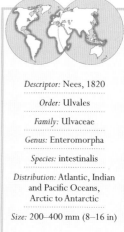

Descriptor: Nees, 1820

Order: Ulvales

Family: Ulvaceae

Genus: Enteromorpha

Species: intestinalis

Distribution: Atlantic, Indian and Pacific Oceans, Arctic to Antarctic

Size: 200–400 mm (8–16 in)

SEA LETTUCE *Ulva lactuca*

Descriptor: Linnaeus, 1753

Class: Chlorophyceae

Order: Ulvales

Family: Ulvaceae

Genus: Ulva

Species: lactuca

Distribution: Worldwide

Size: Up to 180 mm long (7 in)

The Sea Lettuce is so named because it is edible, and in many places it has been collected and eaten since time immemorial – especially in northern Europe and Japan. It is not a particularly robust species, and so is often broken away from its holdfast by the waves; when this happens it does not die, but carries on growing as a floating plant. Sometimes these fragments form large masses, and when these are washed onto the shore, they more or less dominate the shoreline. This can cause significant problems on tourist beaches, as the rotting material has a most unpleasant smell.

Lomentaria articulata RED SEAWEED

R ed Seaweed is a reddish to dark brown algal plant that is distributed along the coasts of the Atlantic and Indian Oceans as far as the Philippines. It is usually found growing in damp places on rocks in the mid- to low littoral zone, but also occurs in the sublittoral to a depth of about 20 metres (66 ft). Sometimes it attaches itself to other seaweeds, especially kelps, but most of the time it forms tight masses on large surfaces. This species typically grows to a maximum size of around 100 mm (4 in), however, in some locations it can reach 250 mm (10 in).

Descriptor: Lyngbye, 1819

Class: Rhodophyceae

Order: Rhodymeniales

Family: Champiaceae

Genus: Lomentaria

Species: articulata

Distribution: Atlantic and Indian Oceans to the Philippines

Size: To 100 mm (4 in)

CORAL WEED *Corallina officinalis*

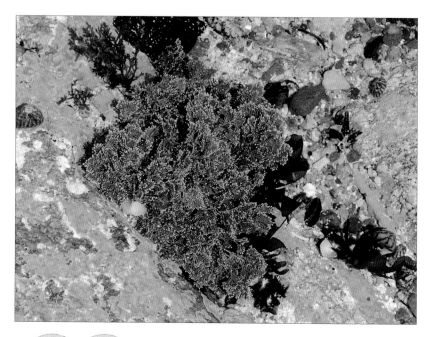

Descriptor: Linnaeus, 1758

Class: Rhodophyceae

Order: Corallinales

Family: Corallinaceae

Genus: Corallina

Species: officinalis

Distribution: Worldwide

Size: To 120 mm (5 in)

A member of the red seaweed family, the Coral Weed is found on almost every coast around the world. It is typically a pinkish colour, but can vary from yellow to purple. Where the light is particularly strong, the finely divided fronds tend to be much paler. This is due to bleaching caused by the sun's ultra-violet radiation. Coral weed usually grows in tidal pools from the mid-littoral zone down to the sublittoral, where it often forms tight clumps that can be quite extensive; these provide valuable refuges for a wide variety of small marine organisms.

Lithophyllum incrustans LAVENDER CORALLINE

The 'Lavender Coralline', *Lithophyllum incrustans* (it has no common name), is a calcareous plant that is found along the coasts of the Atlantic and Indian Oceans, as well as the Mediterranean Sea. It is typically a pink or purple colour, and grows on exposed rocks in the mid- to low littoral zone. Identification can be difficult, as there are several very similar species. Here it is shown growing between patches of coral weed. Mature specimens can grow to around 100 mm (4 in) in diameter, and about 1–2 mm thick. The undulating margins are thickened and have pale edges.

Descriptor: Philippi, 1837

Class: Rhodophyceae

Order: Corallinales

Family: Corallinaceae

Genus: Lithophyllum

Species: incrustans

Distribution: Atlantic and Indian Oceans

Size: 50–75 mm (2–3 in)

LICHEN CORALLINE *Lithophyllum lichenoides*

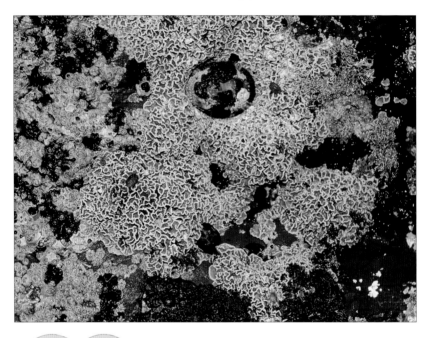

Descriptor: Philippi, 1837

Class: Rhodophyceae

Order: Corallinales

Family: Corallinaceae

Genus: Lithophyllum

Species: lichenoides

Distribution: Atlantic and Mediterranean

Size: 50–75 mm (2–3 in)

The Lichen Coralline, which is an often abundant low-growing calcareous plant, is distributed along the coasts of the north-eastern Atlantic Ocean and the western Mediterranean Sea. It is found in the mid-littoral zone, and is very well attached to the rocks it grows on – these are typically in exposed positions where few other plants could survive. It grows to a thickness of 1–3 mm, and the patches reach around 75 mm (3 in) across; these are divided into lots of small cell-like chambers. The patches often grow into one another, and when this happens, much larger structures are formed.

SPONGES

Kingdom: Animalia Phylum: Porifera; Grant, 1836

Sponges or poriferans, which are the most primitive multicellular animals in existence, are filter feeding organisms that are found in aquatic environments worldwide, ranging from tidal rock pools to sea beds of the deep oceans. Although some are only found in fresh water – about 150 species – around 5,000 others are exclusively marine. Sponges have sessile lifestyles – that is, they live fixed to an object of some description, and they derive nourishment by pumping water through their bodies; as it passes through, any particles are filtered out and digested. Their bodies are extremely simple – they have no true tissues, muscles, nerves or internal organs, and lack a true circulatory system.

SULPHUR SPONGE
Suberites domuncula

Distributed along the coasts of northern Europe and the Mediterranean Sea, the Sulphur Sponge usually lives in the sublittoral zone, where it may reach 300 mm (12 in) in diameter. It is also found in some places in tidal rock pools at the lower edge of the littoral zone. In such instances, it is much smaller, only growing to around 20–30 mm (1 in) in diameter. It is able to flourish without fear of predation because it contains a neurotoxin that is capable of causing death to many marine organisms. This and other chemicals give it a sulphurous smell, hence the origin of its name. It is, however, eaten by the hawksbill turtle, which is immune to the poison.

Descriptor: Olivi, 1792

Class: Demospongiae

Order: Hadromerida

Family: Suberitidae

Genus: Suberites

Species: domuncula

Distribution: Europe & Mediterranean

Size: To 300 mm (12 in)

TRUE WORMS

KINGDOM: ANIMALIA PHYLUM: ANNELIDA
CLASS: POLYCHAETA; GRUBE, 1850

The True Worms or 'polychaetes', are segmented marine worms that can be found in more or less all of the world's oceanic environments, from species that are free floating to those that burrow into the bed of the deep sea. Some live in tubes buried in thick mud, whereas others construct tubes that stand proud of the substrate; still others simply hide beneath rocks or in amongst shingle. A few are parasitic on other marine creatures.

All True Worms have characteristic fleshy structures called 'parapodia' – these carry a number of chitinous bristles called 'chaetae'. There are around 9,000 different species in total, which are divided into about 80 families. Many are so similar that they can only be successfully identified under a microscope. The smallest of the true worms are under a millimetre long; at the other end of the scale, some of the larger ones, such as *Eunice gigantea*, may grow to as much as three metres (10 ft) long. Amongst the more commonly recognized species are ragworms, lugworms, bristleworms and featherduster worms.

LUGWORM *Arenicola marina*

Descriptor: Linnaeus, 1758

Order: Capitellida

Family: Arenicolidae

Genus: Arenicola

Species: marina

Distribution: East coast of United States, Europe, Mediterranean, Indian coasts

Size: To 300 mm (12 in)

The Lugworm is well known to fishermen in many parts of the world as a popular bait. It is distributed along the Atlantic coasts of both the United States and Europe, as well as parts of the Mediterranean Sea and some Indian shorelines. It lives in a 'U'-shaped tunnel that it digs in sand or thick mud, leaving a characteristic worm cast at one end. There are several similar species, with the one shown here – *Arenicola marina* – growing to around 225 mm (9 in), and those from North America reaching 300 mm (12 in). The lugworm feeds by swallowing sand and digesting any edible particles as it passes through – the rest is then expelled as the cast.

Nereis diversicolor RAGWORM

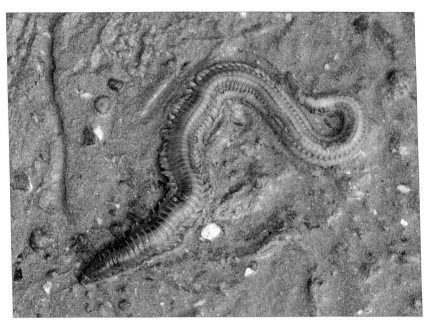

A lso known as the Common Clam Worm or Sandworm, Ragworm is the generic name for many similar species of burrowing polychaetes; there are about 120 in all. They are found worldwide, from the littoral zone to great depths. Although they will eat vegetative matter – especially algae – they are mostly predators, hunting various small invertebrates such as other marine worms. Although they spend a large proportion of their lives underground, they will also swim freely at certain times, such as the run-up to breeding. Their larvae are free-swimming in the plankton, however, once they have grown to a certain stage, they sink to the bottom to begin life as an adult.

Descriptor: Linnaeus, 1758

Class: Polychaeta

Order: Phyllodocida

Family: Nereidae

Genus: Nereis

Species: diversicolor

Distribution: Worldwide

Size: To 250 mm (10 in)

SPLIT-CROWN FEATHER DUSTER *Anamobaea orstedii*

Descriptor: Krøyer, 1856

Order: Canalipalpata;
Suborder: Sabellida

Family: Sabellidae

Genus: Anamobaea

Species: orstedii

Distribution: Tropical Atlantic

Size: Crown to 50 mm (2 in)

The Split-Crown Feather Duster is a tube worm that is distributed throughout the tropical Atlantic Ocean, where it can occur either as a solitary individual or in small groups. It has a crown of feathery gills which are used to filter microscopic planktonic creatures from the surrounding water, and lives in a tube constructed out of grains of sand bonded together with a glue-like secretion. At the first sign of any potential trouble, it instantly withdraws into the tube for safety. This species has a marked division running across the crown, which is the feature that it was named after.

Sabella magnifica PINK & WHITE FEATHER DUSTER

Distributed across the Indo-Pacific Oceans, the Pink and White Feather Duster is a member of a group that is known as the fanworms. This species grows to a crown diameter of around 100 mm (4 in), and has an omnivorous diet, feeding on small planktonic creatures and waterborne marine algae which it traps in its feather-like gills. These particles are then slowly transferred to the mouth where they are consumed. It lives in a tube constructed out of grains of sand or mud bonded together with a glue-like secretion. As its name would suggest, it has a strong pink and white coloration.

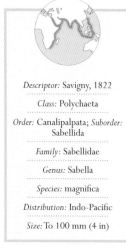

Descriptor: Savigny, 1822

Class: Polychaeta

Order: Canalipalpata; *Suborder:* Sabellida

Family: Sabellidae

Genus: Sabella

Species: magnifica

Distribution: Indo-Pacific

Size: To 100 mm (4 in)

FLOWERING PLANTS

KINGDOM: PLANTAE DIVISION: MAGNOLIOPHYTA
CLASSES: MAGNOLIOPSIDA – DICOTS – LILIOPSIDA – MONOCOTS

The seashore is home to many plants that are not found growing wild anywhere else. The unusual and often harsh prevailing conditions have led to many special adaptations, including a high salt tolerance, the ability to deal with arid soils that are low in nutrients, and the capacity to cope with high winds. They also have to cope with the risk of occasional inundation by sea water. There may be as many as 400,000 different species of flowering plants – also known as 'angiosperms' – with new ones being identified on a regular basis. The most numerous family by a long way are the orchids, with around 25,000 different species. The other large families include the daisies (around 20,000 species), the legumes (16,000 species), the madders (13,000 species) and the grasses (9,000 species). It is thought that flowering plants first evolved around 130 million years ago, although non-flowering terrestrial plants (which reproduced with spores) first arose some 300 million years before this.

SCARLET PIMPERNEL *Anagallis arvensis*

Descriptor: Linnaeus, 1753

Class: Magnoliopsida

Order: Ericales

Family: Myrsinaceae

Genus: Anagallis

Species: arvensis

Distribution: Europe, Asia and North America

Size: 400 mm (16 in) across

Also known as Red Chickweed, Shepherd's Clock and Poor Man's Weather Glass, the Scarlet Pimpernel is an attractive low-growing annual plant that is often found in sandy soils above the tide line. It has small orange-red flowers that only open when the sun is shining – in mid-afternoon, or if bad weather is due, or the petals fold in on themselves, hence the origin of some of the common names. It flowers in the summer, to a height of about 150 mm (6 in) and is distributed across most of Europe, Asia and North America, where it is generally regarded as a weed species.

Armeria maritima SEA THRIFT

The Sea Thrift, which is known by several common names including Sea Pink, is one of the best known flowering plants of temperate seashores. It is distributed throughout the northern hemisphere, and has in recent years become a popular cultivated species in domestic rock gardens. It is a salt-tolerant perennial that grows in large dense clumps, from which long, thin flower stems are produced. At the top of these, a pink flower typically forms, although there are many subspecies and strains which may be white, purple or red. The stems usually reach an overall height of about 250 mm (10 in).

Descriptor: (Mill.) Willd

Class: Magnoliopsida

Order: Caryophyllales

Family: Plumbaginaceae

Genus: Armeria

Species: maritima

Distribution: Temperate northern hemisphere

Size: Height 250 mm (10 in)

HOTTENTOT FIG

Carpobrotus edulis

The Hottentot Fig, which is also known as the Ice Plant or Sour Fig, was originally a native of South Africa; however, mankind has since introduced it worldwide. It was deliberately planted along American railroads at the beginning of the twentieth century to help prevent the soil under the tracks being eroded away. It is extremely tolerant of harsh winds, dry soils and salt-laden air, and so is often able to out-compete the local flora. It can take over vast areas, and many supra-littoral environments are now dominated by this plant. Its invasive ability has put many displaced species on the endangered list. The large flowers, which are popular with insects such as bees, are either pink or yellow.

Descriptor: Linnaeus, 1753

Division: Magnoliophyta

Class: Magnoliopsida

Order: Caryophyllales

Family: Aizoaceae

Genus: Carpobrotus

Species: edulis

Distribution: Originally South African, introduced worldwide

Size: Flowers typically to 150 mm (6 in)

VIPER'S BUGLOSS

Echium vulgare

Viper's Bugloss is a plant that was originally a native of Northern Europe – however, it was introduced to North America and now grows as a weed in many places. It is able to withstand arid conditions, and can be found growing in many beach dune systems in the supra-littoral zone. It flowers from mid-spring to late summer, with the petals starting out pink and then turning to a strong blue as they age. It has long, thin hairy leaves; these are the favoured food for many threatened butterfly and moth species, and so Viper's Bugloss is an important component in a lot of sensitive ecosystems.

Descriptor: Linnaeus

Kingdom: Plantae

Division: Magnoliophyta

Class: Magnoliopsida

Order: Boraginales

Family: Boraginaceae

Genus: Echium

Species: vulgare

Distribution: Northern Europe, introduced to North America

Size: Typically to 800 mm (31 in) in height

SEA HOLLY *Eryngium maritimum*

Descriptor: Linnaeus 1753

Class: Magnoliopsida

Order: Apiales

Family: Apiaceae

Genus: Eryngium

Species: maritimum

Distribution: Europe, North America, Australia

Size: 400–700 mm (16–28 in)

The Sea Holly, which is also known as the Eryngo, Sea Hulver and Cardoon, is distributed along the coasts of Europe, North America (as far south as Mexico), as well as Australia, North Africa and south-west Asia. It is a tough perennial plant with very sharp spines on its leaves that is often found just above the spring high tide line. It has a number of special adaptations that ensure it is able to survive in the arid, salt laden environment, including a thick waxy cuticle and a very long root system which may penetrate to a depth of a metre (3 ft) or more. This makes it a popular plant for improving erosion resistance in unstable soils.

Galium verum LADY'S BEDSTRAW

Lady's Bedstraw, which is also known as Yellow Bedstraw, is distributed across North America and Europe to western Asia. It is an important member of many supra-littoral ecosystems, where it is a larval foodplant for many kinds of insects, including several endangered species. It is a low-growing herbaceous annual that straggles across the ground, producing large numbers of small bright yellow flowers throughout the summer. Where the stems touch the ground, they frequently take root – this helps it to spread quickly , especially where the soil conditions are poor and seeds struggle to germinate.

Descriptor: Linnaeus, 1753

Order: Gentianales

Family: Rubiaceae

Genus: Galium

Species: verum

Distribution: Across North America and Europe to western Asia

Size: To 400 mm (16 in) across and 250 mm (10 in) in height

BIRDSFOOT TREFOIL
Lotus corniculatus

The Birdsfoot Trefoil, which is known as Birdsfoot Deervetch in North America, and Lady's Fingers elsewhere, is a low-growing perennial that is commonly found in the supra-littoral zone close to the high tide line. It has distinctive yellow flower heads that look similar to those of the pea family. These are made up of four to six individual flowers that often have red patches on them; it flowers throughout the summer. The seed pods are typically 20 mm (¾ in) long. It is very tolerant of arid soils, and is an important foodplant for many insects, including several species of blue butterflies.

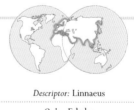

Descriptor: Linnaeus

Order: Fabales

Family: Fabaceae;

Subfamily: Faboideae

Genus: Lotus

Species: corniculatus

Distribution: Temperate Eurasia and North Africa

Size: To around 400 mm (16 in)

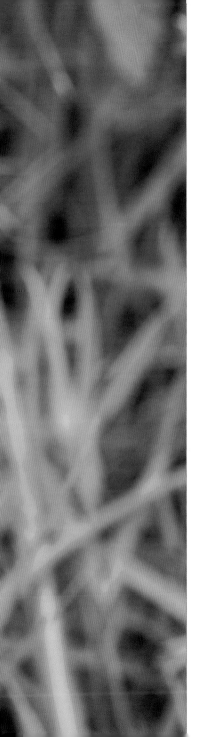

RAGGED ROBIN
Lychnis flos-cuculi

The Ragged Robin is a plant with distinctive pink flowers that is native to Europe, but has been introduced to the north-eastern United States. It is found in damp areas, including in the margins of seashore ecosystems where marshland and dune systems meet. It used to be a common perennial, however, modern agricultural practices have resulted in many of the marshes where it previously thrived being drained. As a result its range has been declining for many years. It flowers from mid-spring to mid-summer; each of the five petals is split into four long thin lobes.

Descriptor: Linnaeus

Order: Caryophyllales

Family: Caryophyllaceae

Genus: Lychnis

Species: flos-cuculi

Distribution: Native to Europe, introduced to northeastern United States

Size: Height typically to 850 mm (33 in)

EUROPEAN WHITE WATERLILY *Nymphaea alba*

Descriptor: Linnaeus, 1753

Order: Nymphaeales

Family: Nymphaeaceae

Genus: Nymphaea

Species: alba

Distribution: Europe, North Africa and Middle East

Size: Leaves to 300 mm (12 in); flowers to 250 mm (10 in)

Also known as the White Lotus, the European White Waterlily is an aquatic plant that is distributed across Europe, North Africa and the Middle East. It is often found in freshwater ponds close to the shoreline, where its floating heart-shaped leaves can dominate the entire surface. These can grow to 300 mm (12 in) in diameter, and are often used by aquatic invertebrates as cover from predators. The large white flowers are produced from separate stalks, and have around 25 petals with a yellow centre. They close at night, re-opening again in the morning.

Oenothera biennis COMMON EVENING PRIMROSE

The Common Evening Primrose, which is also known as the Evening Star or Fever Plant, was originally native to North America; however, it was introduced to Europe later on and now flourishes in many wild places there. It is a biennial that produces vivid yellow flowers, and may reach 1.5 metres (5 ft) in height. The name comes from the fact that the flowers open in the evening – these are produced throughout the summer, and each one only lasts for about a day. These plants are pollinated at night by moths, and during the day by bees.

Descriptor: Linnaeus, 1753

Class: Magnoliopsida

Order: Myrtales

Family: Onagraceae

Genus: Oenothera

Species: biennis

Distribution: Native to North America

Size: 1–1.5 m (3–5 ft)

WILD THYME *Thymus polytrichus*

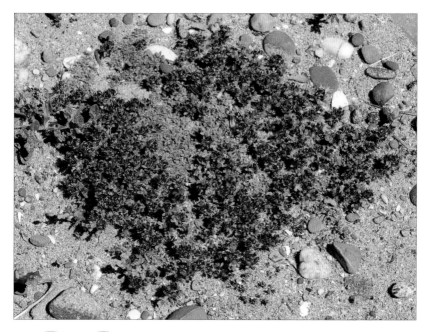

Descriptor: Linnaeus, 1753

Class: Magnoliopsida

Order: Lamiales

Family: Lamiaceae

Genus: Thymus

Species: polytrichus

Distribution: Europe, Asia and North America

Size: To 50 mm (2 in)

Wild Thyme is found throughout Europe, Asia and North America. It can often be found above the high tide line where it is able to withstand the arid soil and harsh conditions that prevail. It is a low-growing evergreen plant that produces large numbers of small pink or purple flowers throughout the summer, and their sweet smell often carries in the air for some distance. These plants are frequently visited by pollinating insects such as bees and butterflies. Wild thyme has small oval leaves that contain fragrant oils; indeed, cultivated thymes are a very popular herb for culinary purposes.

Xanthoria parietina COMMON ORANGE LICHEN

The Common Orange Lichen – also known as Shore Lichen and Maritime Sunburst Lichen – is distributed worldwide, usually growing on rocks, trees or buildings. It is often found on exposed rocks in the splash zone above the high tide mark where no other plants are able to grow. It thrives in nitrogen-rich environments, and does especially well beneath areas where birds roost regularly, as their droppings provide rich nutrients. It forms patches that may reach 100 mm (4 in) in diameter; these are attached to the substrate with fine white hair-like roots. Lichens are able to survive in very harsh conditions, but are very slow growing.

Descriptor: Fries, 1860

Class: Ascomycetes

Order: Teloschistales

Family: Teloschistaceae

Genus: Xanthoria

Species: parietina

Distribution: Worldwide

Size: Patches to 100 mm (4 in)

BIRDS

....

KINGDOM: ANIMALIA PHYLUM: CHORDATA
SUBPHYLUM: VERTEBRATA CLASS: AVES; LINNAEUS, 1758

The birds that are found on the seashore can be divided into two categories – those that are true seabirds, and those that are terrestrial. The former have adapted to life on, or in close proximity to, the sea. Although many seabirds spend most of their lives far out at sea, they all have to return to land to breed. The non-migratory shorebird species often breed in wetland areas, although some such as Oystercatchers nest on sandy beaches, and Common Snipe in meadows and highland areas. Many shorebirds migrate to find the best feeding or breeding areas. A lot fly up to the sub-Arctic and Arctic tundra before the breeding season starts, and then fly south to over-winter in warmer climes before winter returns. The seashore is not just home to seabirds, however, it is also frequented by many terrestrial species. These include everything from skylarks to cuckoos, finches, warblers, magpies, crows, rooks, choughs and pigeons. Where there are prey species, there are almost always predators, too – the sea cliffs are often patrolled by birds or prey such as peregrines and sparrow hawks.

MALLARD *Anas platyrhynchos*

Descriptor: Linnaeus, 1758

Family: Anatidae; *Subfamily:* Anatinae

Genus: Anas

Species: platyrhynchos

Distribution: Central and North America, Europe, Asia. Introduced to Australia and New Zealand

Size: Wingspan to nearly 1 metre (3 ft)

The Mallard has a widespread distribution, being found in the temperate and subtropical regions of Central and North America, Europe and Asia – it has also been introduced to Australia and New Zealand. It is a member of a group known as the 'dabbling ducks', meaning that it feeds by pushing its head underwater and grazing on any vegetation it can reach. Mallards inhabit most places where fresh water is found, including the marshes and estuaries often found along seashore margins. During the winter, many of the northern birds migrate south to warmer areas.

Arenaria interpres RUDDY TURNSTONE

Also known simply as the Turnstone, the Ruddy Turnstone breeds on the high Arctic Tundra during the summer, and then migrates south for the winter, reaching places as far away as South Africa and Australia. In between these journeys it is a common coastal bird in many temperate areas where there are rocky shorelines or seaweed-covered beaches. As the name implies, these birds spend much of their time searching under stones and through debris for small invertebrates such as marine worms, molluscs, amphipods and crustaceans. It will also feed on carrion if the opportunity presents itself.

Descriptor: Linnaeus, 1758

Class: Aves

Order: Charadriiformes

Family: Scolopacidae

Genus: Arenaria

Species: interpres

Distribution: Worldwide

Size: Wingspan to 450 mm
(18 in)

SWAN *Cygnus olor*

Descriptor: Gmelin, 1789

Class: Aves

Order: Anseriformes

Family: Anatidae

Genus: Cygnus

Species: olor

Distribution: Europe, North Africa, Asia and North America

Size: Wingspan to 2.4 m (8 ft)

The Mute Swan is a large white migratory bird that is distributed across the temperate parts of Europe, North Africa, Asia and North America. The males – known as 'cobs' – are larger than the females, which are known as 'pens'. They can reach 1.2 metres (4 ft) in height when standing, and are amongst the heaviest flying birds, typically weighing up to 12 kg (26 lb), although much heavier specimens have been recorded. They have distinctive reddish-orange bills, which makes identification straightforward. Mute Swans often inhabit tidal estuaries and are frequently found in close proximity to the seashore.

Fulmarus glacialis NORTHERN FULMAR

Found on most of the colder seas and oceans of the northern hemisphere, the Northern Fulmar is a member of the petrel family that has been extending its range southwards over the last hundred years or so. It breeds in colonies on cliffs, where it either lays an egg directly onto the rock or makes a slight scrape lined with dead vegetation. Fulmars are superb aerial acrobats, and will often out-manoeuvre gulls when competing for floating carrion. They are great opportunists, and will feed on more or less anything that they can find. They are very long-lived, and can reach around 40 years old.

Descriptor: Linnaeus, 1761

Class: Aves

Order: Procellariiformes

Family: Procellariidae

Genus: Fulmarus

Species: glacialis

Distribution: Oceans and seas of the northern hemisphere

Size: Wingspan to 1.1 m (3½ ft)

EURASIAN OR COMMON PIED OYSTERCATCHER

Haematopus ostralegus

The Eurasian or Common Pied Oystercatcher is a common wader that is found across Europe and Asia as far east as Korea. It is a migratory bird that breeds in northern Europe in the summer, and then flies down to southern Europe and northern Africa for the winter. When they are not breeding, these birds assemble in large flocks, and can often be seen along estuaries and beaches searching for small invertebrates such as marine worms, crabs and molluscs. It is able to open bivalves by prising the halves of the shell apart. It is a distinctive bird with black and white plumage and a bright red bill.

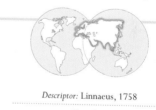

Descriptor: Linnaeus, 1758

Class: Aves

Order: Charadriiformes

Family: Haematopodidae

Genus: Haematopus

Species: ostralegus

Distribution: Across Europe and Asia to Korea

Size: Body length to 440 mm (17 in); Wingspan to 825 mm (33 in)

HERRING GULL

Larus argentatus

The Herring Gull is distributed across most of the northern hemisphere – there are several very similar species, with taxonomists unable to agree on exactly which are distinct species and which are subspecies. Although it is primarily a sea bird, the omnivorous Herring Gull is quick to exploit any easy feeding opportunities, and as such is often seen on refuse tips or following farmers ploughing their fields. Along the seashore it will feed on carrion, as well as any small creatures it can find. The juveniles are marked with brown, whereas the adults have white and grey plumage with a clear red spot on the bill.

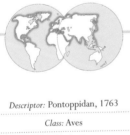

Descriptor: Pontoppidan, 1763	
Class: Aves	
Order: Charadriiformes	
Family: Laridae	
Genus: Larus	
Species: argentatus	
Distribution: Northern hemisphere	
Size: Wingspan to 1.4 m (4½ ft)	

NORTHERN GANNET *Morus bassanus*

Descriptor: Linnaeus, 1758

Class: Aves

Order: Pelecaniformes

Family: Sulidae

Genus: Morus

Species: bassanus

Distribution: North Atlantic

Size: Body length to 1 m (3 ft).
Wingspan to 2 m (6½ ft)

The Northern Gannet is a large migratory seabird that is well known for its incredible plunge-diving abilities when fishing. It is found across the northern parts of the Atlantic Ocean during the breeding season, when it gathers to nest in extensive colonies. These are situated on rocky cliffs, and may be made up of many tens of thousands of individuals. After the season is over, they move southwards for the winter. Adults have a golden-coloured cape and white bodies with black markings, whereas the juveniles are brown. When fully grown, they may have a wingspan of up to two metres (6½ ft).

Pelecanus conspicillatus AUSTRALIAN PELICAN

The Australian Pelican is distributed across Australia, New Zealand and New Guinea as well as across to Fiji and Indonesia. It is a heavily-built bird that when fully grown may have a wingspan of up to 2.5 metres (8 ft), and a body weight of around 10 kg (22 lb). It has a large pink bill, and is found in coastal areas throughout its range, more or less wherever there is sufficient open water for it to catch fish. These pelicans often accumulate in very large flocks – these may be made up of many hundreds or even thousands of individuals.

Descriptor: Temminck, 1824

Order: Pelecaniformes

Family: Pelecanidae

Genus: Pelecanus

Species: conspicillatus

Distribution: Australia and New Guinea to Indonesia and New Zealand

Size: Wingspan to 2.5 m (8 ft)

BROWN OR COMMON PELICAN *Pelecanus occidentalis*

Descriptor: Linnaeus, 1766

Order: Pelecaniformes

Family: Pelecanidae

Genus: Pelecanus

Species: occidentalis

Distribution: Atlantic, Pacific and Gulf Coasts of North and South America

Size: Length to 1.3 m (4ft); wingspan to 2.3 m (7½ ft)

The Brown or Common Pelican is distributed along the Atlantic, Pacific and Gulf Coasts of North and South America. It is the smallest of the seven species of pelican, and although it is somewhat ungainly on land, it is an excellent swimmer with superb eyesight. This species has a slow, powerful flight, and often gathers together in large flocks. It feeds by plunge-diving into shoals of fish from 20 metres (66 ft) or more and then using its massive mouth to engulf several fish at once. During the breeding season, brown pelicans nest in large colonies, where each pair usually produces two or three eggs.

Phalacrocorax carbo GREAT CORMORANT

Also known as the Black Cormorant, the Great Cormorant occurs in several forms – these are distributed from the Atlantic coast of North America across to Europe, Asia, Africa and Australia. One interesting variant of this species is the White-breasted Cormorant, a subspecies from Africa and the Middle East; as its name suggests, it has a much lighter coloured breast than other cormorants. These birds live along estuaries and the seashore, where they feed on various kinds of fish. They catch these by pursuit diving, a form of hunting that is made possible by their ability to stay underwater for significant amounts of time.

Descriptor: Linnaeus, 1758

Class: Aves

Order: Pelecaniformes

Family: Phalacrocoracidae

Genus: Phalacrocorax

Species: carbo

Distribution: Atlantic coast of USA to Europe, Asia, Africa and Australia

Size: To 1 metre (3 ft)

COMMON TERN

Sterna hirundo

The Common Tern is found during the breeding season across the temperate and sub-arctic regions of the northern hemisphere, from North America to Europe and Asia. It feeds on fish which it catches by plunge-diving, and usually nests at ground level in colonies near the shoreline, where two to four eggs are laid. Since these nests are not protected by any natural features such as cliffs, the parent birds become very aggressive, and will repeatedly 'dive-bomb' any potential predators. Once the nestlings have fledged and winter is approaching, it migrates south towards the tropics where it overwinters.

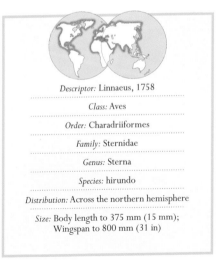

Descriptor: Linnaeus, 1758	
Class: Aves	
Order: Charadriiformes	
Family: Sternidae	
Genus: Sterna	
Species: hirundo	
Distribution: Across the northern hemisphere	
Size: Body length to 375 mm (15 mm); Wingspan to 800 mm (31 in)	

ARCTIC TERN
Sterna paradisaea

The Arctic Tern has a worldwide distribution; during the breeding season, it is found along the coasts of the Arctic and sub-Arctic parts of North America, Europe and Asia. Once it reaches maturity, it forms pair bonds – that is, it mates for life – usually nesting in the same colonies each season. While the eggs and chicks are being fostered, the adult birds become very aggressive, and will attack anything they deem to be a potential threat. When the nestlings have fledged, the adult birds lead them south on the longest migration of any bird – they overwinter near Antarctica, and then return north again the following spring. The Arctic Tern commonly reaches twenty years of age.

Descriptor: Linnaeus, 1758

Class: Aves

Order: Charadriiformes

Family: Sternidae

Genus: Sterna

Species: hirundo

Distribution: Across the northern hemisphere

Size: Body length to 375 mm (15 in);
Wingspan to 800 mm (31 in)

REPTILES

KINGDOM: ANIMALIA PHYLUM: CHORDATA
SUBPHYLUM: VERTEBRATA CLASS: SAUROPSIDA; GOODRICH, 1916

Reptiles of one sort or another may be found almost everywhere, except in the frozen polar regions. Most are predators on small creatures such as insects, frogs and mice, but others – such as tortoises, are exclusively herbivorous. They were the dominant animals on the planet for many millions of years – the vast majority of them died out over time, however, and today there are only around 8,200 species left.

In many tropical regions, some really large reptiles can be found on the seashore – these are the crocodiles, caimans and alligators. A few, especially the Estuarine Crocodile, can be very dangerous. In most other seashore locations, however, the reptiles one is likely to encounter are far more benign. These include snakes, lizards and tortoises, all of which may be found either on the beach itself, or close by it.

Reptiles are ectothermic (cold-blooded) – this means that they cannot make enough heat to keep themselves warm, and so they rely to a very large extent on the warmth of the sun. They are also unable to regulate their internal temperatures.

GREEN SEA TURTLE
Chelonia mydas

The Green Sea Turtle is found in most of the warmer seas and oceans of the world, and usually lives in shallow waters where there are large amounts of seagrass and seaweed, on which it feeds. There are two main groups – those that live in the Atlantic Ocean, and those inhabiting the eastern Pacific Ocean. They are large creatures, reaching 1.5 metres (5 ft) in length, and typically weigh up to 200 kg (440 lb) when fully grown – much larger specimens have occasionally been recorded, however. Maturity is reached at around twenty years of age, and they live to a maximum of about eighty years. Females migrate long distances to lay clutches of up to 200 eggs in nests excavated on suitable beaches.

Descriptor: Linnaeus, 1758

Order: Testudines

Family: Cheloniidae

Genus: Chelonia

Species: mydas

Distribution: Worldwide in tropical, subtropical and warmer temperate waters

Size: To 1.5 m (5 ft) long; Weight typically 200 kg (440 lb), exceptionally to nearly 400 kg (880 lb)

GREEK TORTOISE
Testudo graeca

The Greek Tortoise can be found across parts of southern Europe, western Asia and northern Africa. Within this range, they can be found in many different types of terrain. The individual pictured here was living a few feet from the high tide mark, although in other places they will inhabit mountainous terrain. There are many different subspecies, and taxonomists continue to discover more. The smallest subspecies is the Tunisian Spur-Thighed Tortoise which may weigh less than 0.75 kg (1½ lb), with the largest being from Bulgaria – these can weigh up to 7 kg (15lb). They reproduce by laying eggs, which are laid in specially excavated holes in soft ground – these are then filled in to hide their whereabouts.

Descriptor: Linnaeus, 1758

Class: Sauropsida

Order: Testudines *Suborder:* Cryptodira

Family: Testudinidae

Genus: Testudo

Distribution: Caucasus, North Africa, southern Spain, Sardinia, Turkey, Greece, Macedonia, Bulgaria, Romania

Size: From under 1 kg (2 lb) to 7 kg (15 lb)

SAND LIZARD *Lacerta agilis*

Descriptor: Linnaeus, 1758

Order: Squamata;
Suborder: Sauria

Family: Lacertidae

Genus: Lacerta

Species: agilis

Distribution: Across most of
Europe to Mongolia

Size: To 250 mm (10 in)

The Sand Lizard is found across many parts of Europe and Asia, occurring from the United Kingdom in the west, to Mongolia in the east, and from Sweden in the north, to the Pyrenees in the south. It favours arid and sandy habitats, especially those along coasts, where it is a predator on a wide variety of small invertebrates. The males develop a green coloration during the breeding season, although the degree to which this happens varies across their geographical range. The females dig small burrows in sunny positions, where they lay clutches of up to 14 eggs – these take about two months to develop.

Lacerta viridis GREEN LIZARD

Brightly coloured and conspicuous, the Green Lizard is a relatively large lizard that is found across the warmer parts of Europe, from northern France to the Ukraine, and may reach 380 mm (15 in) in length, including the long tail. It is active during the day, and is often seen close to the shoreline along sunny coasts, where its vivid green coloration makes identification easy. It is omnivorous, taking a wide range of foodstuffs including insects, worms, berries, and even the young of other reptiles or small mammals. Like many other lizard species, this species is able to shed its tail when attacked by a predator.

Descriptor: Laurenti, 1768

Family: Lacertidae

Genus: Lacerta

Species: viridis

Distribution: Across the warmer parts of Europe, from northern France to the Ukraine

Size: Length to 380 mm (15 in)

EUROPEAN ADDER
Vipera berus

Also known as the European Viper, the European Adder is a relatively common and venomous snake that is found throughout Europe and across Asia to China and Korea. It usually inhabits rough ground, and is often seen basking in the sun where heathland, dunes or dry scrub occur along the coast. It is a medium-sized species, typically reaching around 600 mm (24 in) or so, although specimens over one metre (3 ft) have been recorded. Adults feed on various animals, including mice, lizards, amphibians and birds, whereas the young tend to hunt for smaller creatures, such as insects or other invertebrates.

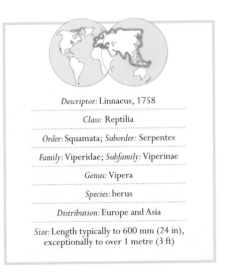

Descriptor: Linnaeus, 1758

Class: Reptilia

Order: Squamata; *Suborder:* Serpentes

Family: Viperidae; *Subfamily:* Viperinae

Genus: Vipera

Species: berus

Distribution: Europe and Asia

Size: Length typically to 600 mm (24 in), exceptionally to over 1 metre (3 ft)

AMPHIBIANS

Kingdom: Animalia Phylum: Chordata
Subphylum: Vertebrata Class: Amphibia; Linnaeus, 1758

There are around 6,000 species of amphibians – this figure is made up of frogs, toads, newts and salamanders. While none of these are marine, they are often found in the seashore environment within a few metres of the high water mark. Where streams and rivers empty into the sea, there are often ponds, marshes and damp places that are home to various kinds of amphibians. Most spend the greater part of the year on land, but with the exception of some species found in rainforest areas, all have to return to water to breed. When the breeding season begins, the mature adults gather in and around ponds, lakes and slow-moving streams where they then mate and lay their eggs. When the eggs hatch, they do so as tadpoles – these have exterior gills and feed on microscopic plants and animals. As they grow, they choose larger food, such as copepods and mosquito larvae. All amphibians are cold-blooded or 'ectothermic', and rely entirely on their surroundings for their body heat. While they normally breathe air, they can also breathe through their skin.

AMERICAN TOAD *Bufo americanus*

Descriptor: Holbrook, 1836

Order: Anura

Family: Bufonidae

Genus: Bufo

Species: americanus

Distribution: Across the eastern
United States and Canada

Size: Length to 100 mm (4 in)

The American Toad, which is distributed across most of the eastern United States and Canada, is often found in areas near ponds and marshes close to the shoreline. In spring, the adult toads seek out fresh water and mate – long strings of eggs are then laid in the form of spawn. These slowly develop into tadpoles, which are only about 50 mm (2 in) long when they first swim free. At this stage, they feed on microscopic algae; however, as they grow, they also start taking small invertebrates. Eventually, they develop legs, lose their tails, and then leave the water in the form of miniature adults.

Bufo bufo COMMON TOAD

Distributed throughout Europe and across Asia eastwards to Siberia, and found as far south as Morocco, the Common Toad is a slow moving amphibian that is often found near the seashore in places where there are freshwater ponds or lakes nearby. It hunts at night, and eats many well known pests including insects and slugs, and is therefore encouraged by most gardeners. It will also take a variety of larger creatures, such as mice, and in most cases it swallows them whole. It has few natural predators, as it is protected by a toxic skin secretion – hedgehogs, however, are immune to this, and frequently kill and eat common toads.

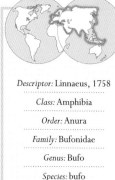

Descriptor: Linnaeus, 1758

Class: Amphibia

Order: Anura

Family: Bufonidae

Genus: Bufo

Species: bufo

Distribution: Across Europe and Asia

Size: Length to 180 mm (7 in)

PEREZI'S OR IBERIAN FROG *Rana perezi*

Descriptor: Seoane, 1885

Order: Anura

Family: Ranidae

Genus: Rana

Species: perezi

Distribution: Across the Iberian peninsula and parts of southern France

Size: To 100 mm (4 in)

The Perezi's or Iberian Frog has mottled markings with a distinctive vivid green background coloration. It is very similar to the Marsh Frog, and can be found in many habitats, including the brackish water of seashore marshes. It is distributed through parts of the Iberian peninsula and southern France, where its characteristic piping calls can be heard for some distance. These are used by adult males for territorial demarcation, as well as for attracting females – the latter tend to be the larger of the two sexes. This species feeds on a wide variety of small creatures.

Rana ridibunda MARSH FROG

The Marsh Frog is found in many parts of Europe as well as Asia as far east as China. It is the largest species found in most parts of its range, and is usually a green colour. Where it lives on a light-coloured substrate such as sand, however, it may be much paler – the individual shown here was photographed living only just above the tide line in a stream bed. Females of this species can grow to a maximum size of around 170 mm (7 in), with the males being significantly smaller at about 120 mm (5 in). This species of frog eats a variety of small creatures, including insects and other small invertebrates.

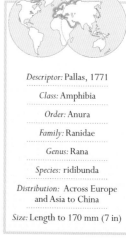

Descriptor: Pallas, 1771

Class: Amphibia

Order: Anura

Family: Ranidae

Genus: Rana

Species: ridibunda

Distribution: Across Europe and Asia to China

Size: Length to 170 mm (7 in)

MAMMALS

KINGDOM: ANIMALIA PHYLUM: CHORDATA
CLASS: MAMMALIA

The mammals that are found at the seashore can be loosely divided into two groups – those that are marine, and those that are terrestrial. The former category includes seals, sealions, dolphins, porpoises and whales, whereas the latter group covers animals like foxes, weasels, mink and rats. Others, such as otters of one species or another, are creatures of both the sea and land. Seals and sealions visit beaches to rest as well as breed. Dolphins, porpoises and whales do not come ashore, but can often be seen close to it. Some whales are plankton feeders, whereas others, along with their smaller relations, the dolphins, feed on fish.

Land mammals, such as foxes and mink, often visit the beach to forage for food – the most numerous, by a long way though, are rats. These hide away during the day, but at night emerge from cover to scavenge for any kind of food they can find, from washed up seaweed to dead animals stranded on the tide line. They will also kill and eat any living animals they find, especially birds, be they eggs, nestlings or adults.

INSECTS
& OTHER INVERTEBRATES

The varied habitats of the seashore are home to many kinds of insects and other invertebrates. These include flies, wasps, beetles, butterflies, moths, spiders, terrestrial worms, slugs, snails, and so on. Some live down on the tide line, feasting on decomposing seaweed or dead animal matter; however, the vast majority live above this in the supra-littoral zone and the areas beyond it. While human activity has forever ruined many natural seashore habitats, some areas are often left as peaceful wildernesses, and can be particularly rich in invertebrates.

The coastal strip is inherently the first land that migrating species meet after crossing the sea, and so can be a very interesting place to examine. Most migrations happen in the summer, with butterflies, moths and dragonflies being the most successful travellers due to their ability to cover vast distances over water. The Monarch butterfly (*Danaus plexippus*) has even crossed the Atlantic Ocean from the United States to parts of Europe on numerous occasions. Many much smaller flying insects are also able to travel far out to sea in search of new lands. These include hover flies, micro moths, wasps, true bugs and others.

SMALL TORTOISESHELL *Aglais urticae*

Descriptor: Linnaeus, 1758

Order: Lepidoptera

Family: Nymphalidae

Genus: Aglais

Species: urticae

Distribution: Across Europe and Asia to China

Size: Wingspan: 45–55 mm (2–2¼ in)

The Small Tortoiseshell is a common butterfly across most of Europe and Asia. It over-winters as an adult – often in quiet places in houses and outbuildings – and is usually one of the first species to be seen flying on sunny days in early spring. The larvae feed on nettles; when the eggs first hatch the young form small communal groups protected by silken nets. As they grow they move away from one another to feed in isolation. Once fully grown, they hang themselves from the underside of a convenient nettle leaf and moult into a pupa, emerging as an adult a week or so later.

Argynnis aglaja DARK GREEN FRITILLARY

Widely distributed across Europe and Asia, the Dark Green Fritillary is a large species of open grasslands. It has a powerful flight, and in its favoured localities can often be seen feeding from a variety of nectar-rich flowers. It has beautifully marked wings – these have an orange background with a network of thin black lines across them. There are several similar species of fritillary, and so obtaining a positive identification can be difficult unless a clear sighting is made. The larvae feed on various members of the violet family.

Descriptor: Linnaeus, 1758

Order: Lepidoptera

Family: Nymphalidae

Genus: Argynnis

Species: aglaja

Distribution: Across Europe to the Arctic Circle, and eastwards over Asia as far as Japan

Size: Wingspan: 58–68 mm (2¼–2½ in)

CINNABAR MOTH
Tyria jacobaeae

The Cinnabar moth is a day flying species that was originally only found in Europe and parts of Asia. These days, however, it is distributed across most of the northern hemisphere as well as in New Zealand and Australia as the result of deliberate introductions. These introductions were brought about by the need to control ragwort, which is extremely toxic to cattle. Since the larvae of this moth can strip a large plant in a remarkably short time, it makes for a very efficient and natural method of control. All the stages of the Cinnabar moth contain toxins, and so both the larvae and adults have bright aposematic warning colours.

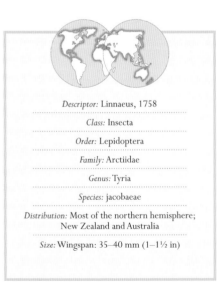

Descriptor: Linnaeus, 1758

Class: Insecta

Order: Lepidoptera

Family: Arctiidae

Genus: Tyria

Species: jacobaeae

Distribution: Most of the northern hemisphere; New Zealand and Australia

Size: Wingspan: 35–40 mm (1–1½ in)

SIX-SPOT BURNET
Zygaena filipendulae

The Six-Spot Burnet moth is widely distributed – although local – throughout Europe from the Mediterranean to the northern shores of Scandinavia. It is a day-flying (diurnal) species that can be locally abundant, especially along coastal margins. The adults – which have a dark blue-black coloration marked with six red spots – can be seen from early summer to mid-autumn. This moth's flight can be somewhat clumsy, making it vulnerable in the air, but it is protected by strong toxins and is generally avoided by predators. The larvae of this species feed on bird's foot trefoil and clover.

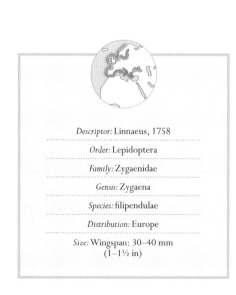

Descriptor: Linnaeus, 1758

Order: Lepidoptera

Family: Zygaenidae

Genus: Zygaena

Species: filipendulae

Distribution: Europe

Size: Wingspan: 30–40 mm
(1–1½ in)

KLAMATH WEED BEETLE *Chrysolina hyperici*

Descriptor: Forster, 1771

Order: Coleoptera

Family: Chrysomelidae

Genus: Chrysolina

Species: hyperici

Distribution: Across northern and central Europe to western Asia; introduced to the US

Size: 5–6 mm
(¼ in)

A small metallic green insect that is sometimes used to help control the klamath weed (also known as St John's Wort), which can be a major agricultural nuisance. It was introduced to the Pacific coast region of the United States for this purpose. The eggs are laid on the undersides of klamath weed leaves, and the night-feeding larvae feed for about a month before pupating underground. This stage lasts just about under two weeks, whereupon the adults emerge. These also feed on leaves and flowers, concentrating on the upright new growth in the spring and moving to the low-growing foliage in wet weather.

Forficula auricularia EUROPEAN EARWIG

Earwigs are insects that belong to the order
Dermaptera – there are about 1,800 species
distributed across 10 families. They are found worldwide,
and none are thought to be harmful in any way, despite
their fearsome tail pincers (*cerci*). The commonest
species in the northern hemisphere is the European
Earwig, having been artificially spread by human activity.
The males can be easily distinguished because they
have longer tail cerci. The females lay their eggs in the
autumn, and then overwinter. In the spring, they guard
over them and then tend the young once they have
hatched. Their diet is very varied, including leaves, fruit,
decomposing plant matter and other insects.

Descriptor: Linnaeus, 1758

Order: Dermaptera

Family: Forficulidae

Genus: Forficula

Species: auricularia

Distribution: Throughout the
northern hemisphere

Size: 12–16 mm
(½–¾ in)

COMMON POND SKATER *Gerris lacustris*

Descriptor: Linnaeus, 1758

Order: Hemiptera

Family: Gerridae

Genus: Gerris

Species: lacustris

Distribution: Across Europe

Size: 20 mm (¾in)

The Common Pond Skater lives on ponds and lakes across Europe. It has specially adapted feet which have a number of water-repelling hairs that provide enough area for it to move across the water without breaking through the surface film. It has very sensitive sense organs that can detect the vibrations of a drowning insect from some distance away. If other prey is not available, it will even eat the young of its own species. It is capable of sustained flight.

Oedipoda caerulescens BLUE-WINGED GRASSHOPPER

The Blue-winged Grasshopper is found across most of Europe, but not on the United Kingdom mainland. It is common in many places, especially dune systems and on other arid soils. The eggs hatch in early summer, and reach sexual maturity in July. When threatened, these grasshoppers jump into the air using their powerful back legs and then glide to safety. When it takes flight its blue-hind wings are very conspicuous; the grasshopper appears like a blue butterfly for a few moments then appears to vanish as it comes to rest.

Descriptor: Linnaeus, 1758

Order: Orthoptera

Family: Acrididae

Genus: Oedipoda

Species: caerulescens

Distribution: Europe; absent from the United Kingdom

Size: 30 mm
(1¼ in)

WATER SCORPION *Nepa cinerea*

Descriptor: Linnaeus, 1758

Order: Hemiptera

Family: Nepidae

Genus: Nepa

Species: cinerea

Distribution: Across Europe

Size: Up to 30 mm (1¼ in)

The Water Scorpion is found across Europe in ponds and streams where it is a voracious predator on a variety of aquatic creatures, ranging from mosquito larvae to tadpoles. The two front legs have evolved into a very effective seizure mechanism; the Water Scorpion waits for suitable prey to swim past, whereupon it snatches the victim and then drags it swiftly to the mouthparts. This insect breathes through its long tail, which at first glance looks like a stinger.

Tipula paludosa EUROPEAN CRANE FLY

The European Crane fly is known by many different local names – these include 'Daddy Long-legs' (although this is also used to refer to certain spiders), 'Jimmy Spinners' and 'mosquito hawks'. The larvae, which live below ground eating the roots of various grasses, are generally known as 'leatherjackets'. Although this is primarily a European species, it has in recent years become established in North America, in parts of Canada and the United States, where it has become a major pest. They can be found more or less anywhere that grasses grow in profusion, including lawns and parklands. The individual pictured here is a female – the sexes can easily be distinguished as the males do not have a pointed tip to the abdomen.

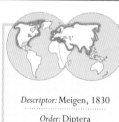

Descriptor: Meigen, 1830

Order: Diptera

Family: Tipulidae

Genus: Tipula

Species: paludosa

Distribution: Across Europe, Asia, the United States and Canada

Size: Body length: 40 mm (1½ in)

HALLOWEEN PENNANT

Celithemis eponina

Also known as the 'Brown-Spotted Yellow-Wing', the Halloween Pennant is quite a small dragonfly that is found near marshes and ponds in Canada, the eastern United States and Mexico, as well as several of the Caribbean islands. The males of this species are not territorial, and they perch near the edge of ponds, waiting for incoming females. Mating typically takes place in the morning. In the more southerly parts of its range, such as Florida, this spectacular species can commonly be seen flying all year round. It has distinctive markings on its wings, which makes identification relatively straightforward.

Descriptor: Drury, 1773

Suborder: Anisoptera

Family: Libellulidae

Genus: Celithemis

Species: eponina

Distribution: Eastern North America, from Canada south to Mexico and the Caribbean

Size: Wingspan: 38–40 mm (1¼–1½ in)

GLOSSARY

Aquatic A creature that lives in water.

Babylon A member of the whelk family which is an active carnivore that preys on other molluscs.

Barnacle Small sessile crustaceans that can be found in intertidal zones worldwide.

Bivalve Molluscs with two separate parts to their shells – examples include mussels, scallops and clams. They are filter feeders on floating particles or microscopic creatures.

Brittle Star Marine animals that look like starfish with long, thin, flexible arms, but are members of a distinct class of echinoderms. They live by filter feeding, scavenging, feeding off decaying animal and plant matter, or predating on small creatures such as shrimps or marine worms.

Brood A generation of young.

Cephalopod A group of marine animals that contain the squid, cuttlefish, nautilus and octopus.

Chitons Marine gastropods that are sometimes called coat-of-mail shells and are occasionally found attached to the underside of rocks in pools.

Cockle A bivalve that burrows into the sea bed and feeds on plankton filtered from the surrounding water.

Cowry A marine gastropod that lives on rocky ground and feeds by browsing on algae and other sessile organisms such as sponges.

Crab Hard-shelled crustaceans that usually have powerful claws and are found across the world. They typically prey on invertebrates such as other crabs, as well as marine worms and molluscs.

Crustacean A group of mostly marine arthropods that includes crabs, lobsters, shrimp, prawns and barnacles as well as terrestrial woodlice, all of which have hard external coverings known as exoskeletons.

Cuttlefish A cephalopod predator with eight arms and two tentacles, as well as excellent vision, which is best known for the white cuttlebones used in the pet trade to provide calcium for caged birds.

Ecdysis The process whereby a crustacean sheds its skeleton between moults.

Echinoderm A large group of marine animals that include the starfish (sea stars), sea urchins, crinoids, sea cucumbers and brittle stars.

Exoskeleton The hard outer skeleton of an animal such as an insect or crustacean.

Feather-star Marine animals that are also referred to as crinoids or sea lilies and which appear at first sight to be plants. Their diet is composed of minute planktonic creatures which they filter from the surrounding water.

Gastropods A class of molluscs that include land and marine snails as well as slugs.

Hermit Crab Marine crustaceans that live in discarded seashells.

Horseshoe Crab A marine animal that belongs to the subphylum Chelicerata. It eats a variety of small marine invertebrates, including molluscs, shrimps and polychaete worms, and is often described as a living fossil.

Intertidal Zone *See* Littoral Zone.

Jellyfish Marine animals which belong to the class Scyphozoa and feed on small fish, crustaceans and plankton. These are caught with long tentacles that are equipped with large numbers of stinging cells.

Limpet A marine gastropod that is found in the intertidal zone attached to rocks, where it is able to hold fast with a strong muscular foot. It feeds on marine algae.

Littoral Zone The area that lies between the high water and low water marks.

Lobster Large marine crustaceans that are predators which feed on any creatures they can catch and overpower.

Mandible An animal's jaw.

Metamorphosis The process whereby an animal changes from one stage to another, such as from nauplius to adult.

Moult The process whereby an animal sheds its skin.

Murex A gastropod found on reefs or flat sandy areas in warm and tropical waters where it is a predator on other molluscs as well as sponges and other small invertebrates. Often equipped with sharp spines.

Mussel A bivalve with a dark blue coloured shell that can be found in large beds in both temperate and polar waters, where it feeds by filtering plankton from the surrounding water.

Nautilus A nocturnal cephalopod that looks similar to a large gastropod and is found in the waters of the Indian and south-western Pacific Oceans.

Nocturnal An organism that is active at night.

Nudibranch Marine gastropods that are commonly known as sea slugs. Some have powerful toxin defences and advertise their unpalatability with bright aposematic warning colours.

Octopus A soft-bodied cephalopod predator with a characteristic shape and eight powerful arms.

Oviparous An animal that lays its eggs outside its body.

Periwinkle A marine gastropod that is found on rocks and in tidal pools, where it feeds on algae which it rasps away from hard surfaces using its radula. Often has a very variable coloration.

Polychaete Worm These are segmented marine worms that can be found in more or less all of the world's oceanic environments.

Prawn A common marine crustacean that is found in all the world's seas and oceans and feeds on small particles of food that may be either plant or animal in origin.

Predator An animal that feeds by killing and eating other animals.

Queen Conch A large marine gastropod that is also called 'Caribbean Queen Conch' and 'Pink Conch', found in Neotropical Atlantic waters off the coasts of Florida, southern Mexico, Venezuela, Brazil, and the Caribbean, where it feeds on algae.

Razor Shells Marine bivalves that have elongated shells and are found across the northern hemisphere in shallow water along many of the Atlantic and Pacific coasts, where they burrow into sand or coarse mud in the lower tidal and upper sublittoral zones. They are collected in some areas for fishing bait or human consumption.

Sand-hopper Small nocturnal amphipods that move around by hopping, and are found in the upper littoral zone, where they feed at night on stranded seaweed.

Scallop A marine bivalve that has the ability to swim freely.

Sea Anemone Marine animals that belong to the Class Anthozoa and have specialized stinging cells called nematocysts on the ends of their tentacles – these are used to help capture prey.

Sea Cucumber Marine animals that are in the same phylum grouping as starfish and sea urchins, and usually feed by scavenging on sea bed detritus as well as plankton, and move around using small tube feet.

Seahorse A group of small fish with extremely unusual physical forms and life histories that usually hide amongst thick seaweed or in rocky crevices, where they quietly feed on small invertebrates.

Sea Slater Small nocturnal crustaceans that are found in the upper littoral zone and feed on seaweed and any edible matter that has been washed ashore by the tide.

Sea Urchin Marine animals that are closely related to starfish and brittle stars and have an omnivorous diet that is composed of seaweed, algae, sponges, barnacles and molluscs as well as any dead creatures that they come across.

Seaweed A group of large, multicellular algae that are mostly found in the littoral and upper sublittoral zones on rocky ground.

Social Animals that live in organized groups.

Spider Conch Marine gastropods with heavy shells that have long, curved arm-like features. Found in shallow reef areas throughout the Indo-West Pacific region. Often harvested for food and for the decorative qualities of their shells.

Squat Lobster Marine crustaceans that are closely related to hermit crabs.

Squid A cephalopod predator that has eight arms and two tentacles, as well as excellent vision and is found in seas and oceans across the world where it feeds on fish and other small creatures.

Starfish Marine animals that are also known as sea stars and have a central body with, most commonly, five radial arms. Some feed on coral polyps, others on decaying plant or animal matter. Most will also attack and eat more or less any creature they can subdue.

Sublittoral Zone The zone that lies just below the low water mark.

Supra-Littoral Zone The zone immediately above the highest tide line.

Top Shells Common marine gastropods that are found in rocky tidal pools with a good covering of seaweeds, where they feed on various small creatures such as hydroids.

Triton A large marine gastropod that is a very active predator and found in the Indo-West Pacific down to depths of about 40 metres (131 ft).

Viviparous The term used to describe giving birth to live young.

Whelk A marine gastropod that is collected commercially in traps for the food trade.

INDEX

PICTURE CREDITS

The author and publishers would like to thank the following individuals and organizations for the kind use of their photographs in this book. The pictures are credited in the order in which they appear in the book.

p10 Tino Smith; pp12, 13, 14 Digital Vision; p15 Patrick Hook; p16 Digital Vision; pp17, 18 Patrick Hook; p19 Digital Vision; p20 Daniel Buswell; p21 Patrick Hook; p23 Digital Vision; p26 Patrick Hook; pp28, 29 Digital Vision; p30 top Oneworld-images, bottom Patrick Hook; pp32, 33 Valérian Rossigneux; p34 Stephen Bonk; p35 Chad Koski; pp36, 37 Patrick Hook;